THE COMPLETE
WEDDING
PLANNER

Edith Gilbert

Meadowbrook Press

Library of Congress Cataloging-in-Publication Data
Gilbert, Edith.
　　　The complete wedding planner / Edith Gilbert. — Rev. ed.
　　　　　p. cm.
　　　ISBN 0-88166-355-7
　　　1. Wedding etiquette.　2. Weddings—planning.　I. Title.
BJ2051.G46　1999
395.2'2—dc21　　　　　　　　　　　　　　　　99-23697
　　　　　　　　　　　　　　　　　　　　　　　　CIP

Editor: Christine Zuchora-Walske
Copyeditor: Nancy Baldrica
Proofreader: Joseph Gredler
Production Manager: Joe Gagne
Desktop Publishing: Danielle White
Cover Photo: Lilo Raymond
Illustrations: Terri Mitchelson

Published by Meadowbrook Press, 5451 Smetana Drive, Minnetonka, Minnesota 55343.

www.meadowbrookpress.com

03　02　01　00　99　　　　10　9　8　7　6　5　4　3　2　1

Printed in the United States of America

Acknowledgments

I deeply appreciate the helpful suggestions and guidance that was so generously given to me by members of the clergy as I revised my book.

My heartfelt thanks go to the Reverend Philip Schairbaum, the First Congregational Church, Charlevoix, Michigan; to the late Dr. Richard C. Hertz, Rabbi Emeritus, Temple Beth El, Birmingham, Michigan; to Father Elias Koppert, O.P. M., Holy Childhood Church, Harbor Springs, Michigan; and to Senior Rabbi Samuel E. Karff, D.H.L., Congregation Beth Israel, Houston, Texas.

Revisions

When *The Complete Wedding Planner* was originally published in 1983, it was the first book to speak to the bride and groom as a couple, instead of addressing only the bride and her mother, as had been done in the past. It is still my strong desire to share with the bride and groom the most complete, up-to-date, and detailed information on the entire subject of weddings in this second updated and revised edition.

The etiquette questions I received in the past through my newspaper column cannot compare with the thousands of e-mail etiquette questions that have crossed my computer this year—for the latter are more open, more concerned, and sometimes more heart-rending than any I've heard before.

Naturally, many questions pertain to second marriages and stepparents: Who should walk the bride down the aisle? How can children from a former marriage be involved in the wedding ceremony? How should a wedding invitation be worded when several family members will host the wedding? Where should a biological parent of an adopted bride, or divorced parents, be seated during the ceremony and reception?

Many of these, as well as more complicated questions, have been answered in this book. Previous information has been expanded, details have been greatly embellished, and more examples cited.

I am deeply grateful to the wise and helpful counsel of Jeannie Babbitt of Sweet Creations and the State Representative of the International Cake Exploration Society; to Jill Leetsma, a member of the Professional Association of Custom Clothiers; to my friends, the Paul Westons, who enlightened me on the subject of Asian weddings; and to Nancy Porter and Allan Warner, who often acted as sounding boards.

I sincerely hope that this newly revised edition will be even more helpful in making your wedding go smoothly by saving you an enormous amount of time and energy and by giving you the comfort of knowing that you have covered everything.

Contents

Chapter Three: Preparing for Marriage

Chapter Four: The Wedding Budget and Calendar

Chapter Five: Planning the Wedding and Honeymoon

Chapter Six: Planning the Reception

Chapter Seven: Stationery

Chapter Eight: Attendants in the Wedding Party

Chapter Nine: What to Wear

Chapter Ten: Flowers

Chapter Eleven: The Sound of Music

Chapter Twelve: Photographs and Videotapes

Chapter Thirteen: Gifts

Chapter Fourteen: Transportation

Chapter Fifteen: The Rehearsal and Ceremony

Chapter Sixteen: The Wedding Day

How to Use This Book Wisely

Love does not consist in gazing at each other,
but in looking outward in the same direction.

ANTOINE DE SAINT-EXUPÉRY

No matter what your age, your background, or your career, or even whether you have been married before (30 percent of today's marriages are second weddings), you need to know when to have your wedding, where to have it, who will officiate, how many guests to invite, what to wear, whether to have a rehearsal, and how much the reception will cost. Of course, you will want everything to go smoothly. I have designed this book to help you clear the hurdles along the way.

To use the information in this book effectively, I suggest that you underline the sections that fit your special needs and add any comments you wish—Yes! No! Maybe? Then, let your partner do the same with a pen of a different color. When you are done, the book will be well marked, it's true, but you will have reached numerous important decisions jointly, and the two of you will have an accurate record for easy reference.

If your family is like most families these days, you, your fiancé(e), and both sets of parents may live in different cities, states, or even countries. To make communication simpler, give your parents or members of the wedding party their own copies of this book to consult. The price of one telephone call may cover the cost of that extra copy.

It is time now to knuckle down with a pen in hand and make plans for your perfect wedding. Remember that all weddings are similar, but no two weddings are exactly alike!

My personal wish is that all your private dreams come true!

Edith Gilbert

Chapter One

Getting Off to a Good Start

Manners are the happy way of doing things.

RALPH WALDO EMERSON

Your wedding is going to be the loveliest, smoothest, most memorable wedding ever—just the kind you've both always dreamed it would be! Calm, cool and confident is the way to feel as you prepare for this happy day!

A wedding is not only a joyous occasion to share with family and friends, but also an important ceremonial event and, as such, follows a prescribed form. In spite of some restrictions, you may be surprised and delighted at the great variety of choices open to brides and grooms. Many decisions will reflect your personal tastes, and consequently, your wedding will be unlike any other, while still essentially following tradition.

Over the years wedding ceremonies have changed dramatically. Today, many couples personalize their weddings by writing their own vows. They want to express their own ideas about love and faith while keeping some traditional aspects of the wedding ceremony. Since much time and personal thought goes into this effort, some couples have wedding booklets printed as souvenirs for their guests.

Some couples compose their own words and music for guitar, while some choose contemporary songs to be sung, and others cling to traditional wedding music. Some couples carefully select poems to be read during the ceremony. Some couples design their own invitations or wedding cakes. Weddings are adapting to our current attitudes and lifestyles, and I expect they will continue to do so in the future.

The one thing that never changes, however, is tender human feelings. When planning a wedding, there are so many emotionally-involved people on both sides of the family that it is wise to consider their sensitivities and put yourselves in their shoes. True, every couple contemplating marriage is deeply involved in their own intense feelings, and rightly so! Yet, to prevent any misunderstandings, some guidelines have been developed that are not designed to plague you, but rather to assist you and make your job smoother and less complicated. If at any time these guidelines interfere with your ability to be kind, thoughtful, and considerate, they should be modified to accommodate the present situation.

Wouldn't it be wonderful if everyone could readily understand how we arrived at our decisions! Unfortunately, this is not always so. Customs vary around the country. Seven o'clock may be a very chic time to have a candle-light service in Washington, D.C., but an impractical time among dairy farmers, who finish milking at dusk. There are also great contrasts among religious and ethnic groups. What one group takes for granted, another group may find quite strange. It is hoped that both families graciously accept differences in ceremonial and social customs.

Sometimes, there are three or four generations involved in a wedding, and it may be difficult for the older generation to adapt to new and different ways of doing things. When the younger generation wishes to be innovative, they may need to consider and respect the feelings of kindly relatives and be open to compromise on unimportant details.

Dear Edith,
Our family seems to have a lot of opinions regarding our wedding plans.
Isn't this supposed to be OUR wedding—shouldn't these be OUR decisions?

ANSWER: Yes, it is your wedding, and as time goes by, you will probably make more decisions than you care to make. You will choose where and when your marriage takes place, the vows, the music, your attendants, the style of dress for yourselves and the wedding party, the type of flowers, the number of guests, the wording of the invitations and announcements, the time and place of the reception, the choice of refreshments, the flavor of the cake, the photographer, the gifts for the attendants, the mode of transportation, and of course, the place for your honeymoon.

Your family, however, needs to be consulted early on some of the major decisions affecting them, such as where and when the wedding is to take place. For example, if your brother is graduating from college, you don't want to plan your wedding during his graduation weekend.

For all the above reasons, friendly communication should be developed early between the families of the bride and groom—especcially when step-parents or stepchildren are involved. Thorny etiquette questions may arise that could test the wisdom of Solomon. During a particularly touchy period in a friend's life, I was asked, "How far does one go?" My answer was, "All the way!" To go all the way in handling a new or difficult situation may be the most fruitful decision a couple can make together.

Accept Help When Offered

To guarantee that this experience will be joyful and uplifting, do accept any help that is offered by family and friends. It takes teamwork to orchestrate the numerous details. If someone asks what he or she can do to help, be prepared to tell him or her! If a friend has lovely handwriting, you may ask for help in addressing envelopes for the invitations and/or announcements. If a neighbor is skilled at arranging flowers, ask if he or she will help on the day of the reception. If you need someone to provide transportation for out-of-town guests, let a family member play the roll of chauffeur. Everyone enjoys being caught up in the excitement of a wedding.

Assign Honor Roles

Make an effort to include special members of the family. Honor a favorite aunt or uncle, stepparent, grandparent, or cousin by asking him or her to perform a special duty at the reception. Not only will these people feel flattered by your request, they will provide helpful service at the reception. These assignments will also free the wedding party to enjoy themselves at the reception. Any of the following duties are suitable for consideration:

• Receiving and recording gifts at the reception
• Supervising the signing of the guest book
• Serving or supervising at the punch or refreshment table
• Serving or supervising at the cutting of the wedding cake
• Mingling with and introducing guests
• Assisting the photographer in identifying special guests
• Acting as master of ceremonies on the dance floor
• Directing transportation

You may also invite a special relative or friend to recite a reading during your ceremony. For reading ideas, refer to *Centuries of Writing and Rituals on Love and Marriage* by Eleanor Munro (Penguin) and *Into a Garden: A Wedding Anthology* edited by Robert Hass and Stephen Mitchell (HarperCollins).

The Marriage License

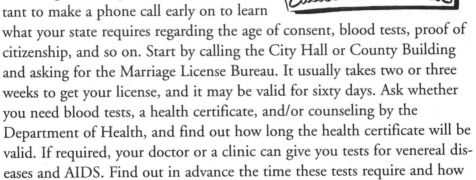

Don't forget the paperwork! Since each state has its own requirements for obtaining a marriage license, it is important to make a phone call early on to learn what your state requires regarding the age of consent, blood tests, proof of citizenship, and so on. Start by calling the City Hall or County Building and asking for the Marriage License Bureau. It usually takes two or three weeks to get your license, and it may be valid for sixty days. Ask whether you need blood tests, a health certificate, and/or counseling by the Department of Health, and find out how long the health certificate will be valid. If required, your doctor or a clinic can give you tests for venereal diseases and AIDS. Find out in advance the time these tests require and how much they cost.

Also, ask about the age of consent in case you will need to obtain a birth certificate or parental consent. If you were not born in the United States, you may need proof of citizenship. If one of you is divorced or widowed, you will need a divorce decree or death certificate.

Making Decisions

Although you might find it difficult to suddenly have to make so many important decisions, you might also find that you have a sincere desire to please everyone and not to hurt anyone's feelings. This is natural. When kind people offer unsolicited or inaccurate advice, many couples respond by saying, "That's nice, but we are going according to the book. We have talked this over with our minister and our wedding coordinator and have reached a decision."

There are times—especially when planning a wedding—when you need to remember the wise counsel given to us by Abraham Lincoln: "You can please some of the people some of the time, but you can't please all of the people all of the time." It's good to listen to the experts first and then do whatever you want.

Hasty Decisions

It is only natural for a couple in their high spirit of enthusiasm to sometimes make hasty decisions, which upon second thought may seem unwise. Too many of my e-mail questions pertain to uninviting a bridesmaid who has moved out of state and canceling a caterer because a better one has been found.

When pressured to make a decision that has not been carefully considered by both the bride and groom, it is best to say, "We'll give it some thought" or "That's a good idea; we'll think it over."

What to Call Your In-Laws

I clearly recall when I became engaged how puzzled I was about what to call my new mother- and father-in-law. Although I admired both enormously, and a warm friendship had developed, I could not bring myself to call them Mother or Father. As it turned out, I had no problem calling my father-in-law Dad, since I never called my own father Dad; and fortunately, my mother-in-law was also a grandmother who was already called Dearie, so it was easy for me to call her by that name, too.

The question of what to call your in-laws is real when you become engaged, since one cannot go around calling out "Hey, you!"

If your future in-laws don't bring up the subject by asking you to call them by their first names, or if they suggest using nicknames, or if you don't wish to call them by the same names their son or daughter calls them (Mom and Dad), ask your fiancé(e) to bring up the subject with them privately. You might also ask them yourself, "Have you thought about what you would like me to call you?"

Will you become a stepparent upon marriage? It is quite common nowadays for stepparents to be called by their first names, unless they prefer otherwise. When a very young child's biological parent is living, it is difficult for him or her to call a stepparent Mommy or Daddy. In this case, if desired, the stepparent can be called Mumsie or Popsie or some other nickname.

Notes

Chapter Two

The Engagement, Showers, and Prewedding Parties

There is no remedy for love than to love more.

HENRY DAVID THOREAU

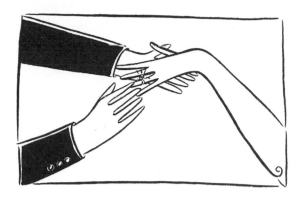

It is wonderful to be engaged! It is also true that a young couple may have mixed feelings about their engagement—one minute they want to keep the delicious secret to themselves, and the next minute they want everyone to know!

Most parents probably will not be surprised to hear the good news, because chances are, they have been well aware of the flowering relationship. Still, it is a courtesy for the young man and woman to have that *special* talk with Mother and Father.

The ideal length for an engagement, if one is planning a traditional wedding, is at least six months, as it takes that much time to comfortably make all the necessary arrangements. Many couples are engaged for a year or more, but for an informal home or garden wedding and reception, three months or less—depending on various circumstances—will do nicely. The engagement may be announced in the newspaper, accompanied by a photograph of the bride or the couple.

Couples who intend to get married in the immediate future, who have been living together for some time, or who are marrying for the second time may prefer to forego the formalities of newspaper engagement announcements and parties. Instead, they will probably announce the wedding date to their family and friends at an informal gathering.

Once a couple is engaged, the man is referred to as the fiancé and the woman is called the fiancée. Both words are borrowed from the French and are pronounced the same way. They indicate that a couple is formally engaged and a public announcement has been made to friends and relatives.

The Engagement Ring

When selecting engagement and wedding rings, keep your budget firmly in mind. There's no need to feel pressured to buy an engagement ring right away. It's possible to combine the engagement and wedding rings, as many people do, in one wide band inset with small diamonds or other stones.

Some couples put off getting an engagement ring for years, until they celebrate a special anniversary. This gift can be just as meaningful then as now—perhaps more so.

Although the diamond is usually considered traditional for an engagement ring, any stone, such as the bride or groom's birthstone, is just as appropriate. An antique ring or treasured family heirloom may be handed down to the bride. If she has a ring or stone in her family, it is also quite proper for the bride to select a setting and for the groom to have the stone reset at his own expense.

Birthstones	
January	Garnet
February	Amethyst
March	Aquamarine
April	Diamond
May	Emerald
June	Pearl
July	Ruby
August	Sardonyx or Peridot
September	Sapphire
October	Opal or Tourmaline
November	Topaz
December	Turquoise or Zircon

Jewelers often sell the engagement and wedding ring in a set made of the same material, because the two rings should fit comfortably on one finger. When the bride and groom visit the jeweler, the bride should be sure to try on both rings to see how they look and feel on her hand before making a selection.

When looking for a reliable jeweler, try to deal with one who is a certified gemologist with a certificate from the Gemological Institute of America. This is the leading authority on diamonds in the United States. Jewelry stores that have been in business for many years have trained staff to help you make a sound choice. They will explain the differences in carat weight, clarity, color, and cut, which determine the price of each stone. (These factors are known as the Four Cs.) In addition, you will be supplied with an appraisal certifying the quality for insurance purposes.

There are also various shapes to consider when choosing a diamond ring:

| Marquis | Pear | Round/Brilliant | Oval | Emerald Cut |

Insurance

If the ring is particularly valuable, it should be insured. Many insurance companies do not like to insure expensive rings and will do so only if a ring is part of a household or other insurance policy. Some companies are known to include clauses in small print that disclaim responsibility for items such as engagement rings. Some insurance companies will only replace a lost or stolen ring at the appraisal value, which may in time be a lot less than its replacement value. Another common loophole is for the company to insure the entire ring if it is lost; if only the stone is lost, the company may claim it is not liable! Read the fine print carefully, and if it is not possible to get the coverage needed, go to another company. An added protection is to take a good close-up photograph of your ring with a description. Specify on the back of the picture the cut, carats, and color of the diamond to be insured.

Rings for a Second Marriage

What does a bride do with engagement and wedding rings from a first marriage? If there are children from a former marriage, these rings are usually kept for them. Otherwise, the first engagement ring may be reset in a new design and worn as a dinner ring.

Engraving the Wedding Band

The wedding band is usually engraved on the inside, although the engagement ring is not. A month or more before the wedding, arrangements should be made to have the ring engraved. Usual inscriptions on the bride's ring are the groom's initials first, then the bride's initials and the date. If the band is wide enough, there may be room for a brief, appropriate sentiment.

The groom's wedding band, if engraved, has the bride's initials first, then his initials and the date. If desired, any meaningful phrase may also be included.

Announcing the Engagement to the Family

After the parents have been told, the first people to tell of your engagement are close relatives and friends. If possible, it is fun to make the announcement at a family gathering, so everyone can hear the good news at the same time and share your happiness.

If you have not met your fiancé(e)'s parents, this is the time to do so. The next step is to have both sets of parents meet or write each other. It is customary and friendly, but not mandatory, for the groom's parents to contact the bride's parents and welcome their daughter as a member of the family. I feel that one should not stand on ceremony, and that the sooner communication is opened up between the sets of parents the better! It may take time for all the parents to get accustomed to the idea of your marriage, so you may need to exercise a little patience before you begin discussing definite wedding plans or setting a date.

Before planning a newspaper release, it is considerate to telephone or write a note to relatives and old friends of both families. It is especially considerate to call on people who are elderly or invalid. Everyone is interested in a wedding and would like to hear it first from you!

Engagement Parties

Where there's room in the heart
there is room in the house.
DANISH PROVERB

Most families become very enthusiastic at the prospect of a wedding, and the bride's parents or a relative may wish to announce the engagement officially at a luncheon, tea, cocktail buffet, or sit-down dinner. This party may take place in the home, at a private club, or in a restaurant, but not in a nightclub! There is usually an element of surprise and no mention is made of the forthcoming announcement on the invitation. After all the guests are assembled, the bride's father or a close relative announces the engagement by standing and proposing a toast such as: "Please join me in a toast to my daughter, Jennifer, and let us welcome the newest member, Bob, to our family." The groom then stands and responds with a toast to the bride and her parents by saying something like this: "I don't have to tell you how lucky I am to become a part of this wonderful family! Jennifer and I want to thank you for being here and for your good wishes."

If the bride's parents live too far away, there is no reason why the groom's parents cannot give the engagement party. When both sets of parents live in the same city, they may choose to cohost the party, or the couple themselves may plan a small, informal gathering to introduce friends and relatives to each other.

There are innumerable ways to break the news at the party, and your own good taste and imagination may provide several novel or interesting ideas. Cocktail napkins with the couple's name, a decorated cake, mints, or blown-up photographs of the couple are only a few suggestions.

Second Marriage

Before a couple announces their engagement publicly, it is a courtesy for widows and widowers to inform their former in-laws of an impending second marriage. It is preferable to write a short note than to telephone, because it may be difficult for former in-laws to handle the unexpected news gracefully. But given a little time, they may give the news of a second marriage their genuine blessing. They may be invited to the wedding, but they do not sit in the reserved section.

When there is an amicable divorce, the same courtesy holds true, especially where children are involved. The former spouse and in-laws are informed of the new circumstances, but are usually not invited to the wedding.

Newspaper Announcements and Photos

A newspaper announcement is easy to prepare. Many papers have forms to be filled out, or you may type the copy, double spaced, on 8½-by-11-inch white bond paper. In the upper right corner list the name, address, and telephone number of the person the newspaper is to contact for additional information. In the upper left corner type "FOR IMMEDIATE

RELEASE" or give a definite release date. Address to the Society Editor, using his or her name if possible.

Immediately below this line, type a brief headline that tells the editor at a glance what the story is about. For example: "Jennifer Lovejoy Engaged to Robert Baldwin".

The newspaper announcement should read something like this:

*Mr. and Mrs. Loren Jay Lovejoy of Harbor Springs announce
the engagement of their daughter, Jennifer, to Mr. Robert Baldwin,
son of Dr. and Mrs. Curtis William Baldwin of Lake Forest, Illinois.*

If the bride's parents are divorced, either parent may announce the engagement. If the mother makes the announcement, the father must be mentioned in the story. When one or both parents are deceased, a close relative, guardian, or friend may announce the engagement. The word "late" should then precede any reference made to either of the deceased parents. If the mother is deceased and the father has remarried, the announcement could simply read as follows:

*Mr. and Mrs. Roger Smith of Mt. Vernon, New York,
announce the engagement of Mr. Smith's daughter, Diane Alice,
to Bruce George Compton.*

Or, it is quite proper for a woman to announce her engagement herself, as follows:

*Miss Alyce Rogers has announced her engagement to
Mr. Hans William Bennett.*

If a woman has been married before, she may use either her maiden name or previous married name, whichever is better known to her friends. When the woman has a medical title, it is abbreviated, such as "Dr. Margot Smith," and it may be used in newspaper announcements only if the bride announces her own engagement. If her parents issue the announcement, her title is not used—for instance: "their daughter, Margot Smith." Later, when her profession is mentioned, she is referred to as "Dr. Smith."

The second paragraph lists more information about the bride—her school, clubs, sorority, and other affiliations and, if she is employed, the name of the firm (optional).

The third paragraph gives information about the groom. It names his parents and where they live. If the parents are divorced, it should read:

Mr. Bruce George Compton is the son of
Mrs. Robert MacArthur of Berkeley, California, and
Mr. Carl Compton of Anaheim, California.

The groom's schools and possibly his job title and the name of his company are mentioned, as well as any past military rank or branch of the service in which he has served. The names of clubs, fraternities, and other affiliations are also listed.

The fourth paragraph could mention the names of grandparents, especially if they are well known. It is not, however, in good taste to list all the parents' or grandparents' achievements in such a way as to detract from the engagement announcement. The following comments are sufficient, for example:

The grandparents of the prospective bridegroom reside in
Washington, D.C., where Judge Compton is a member of the
Supreme Court.

If you feel that the married women mentioned in your announcement would prefer to be called by their own first names, then do so. You may choose to use this method with other announcements or invitations, too:

Mr. James and Mrs. Kathleen Martin announce . . .

The final paragraph may mention the couple's future plans either in a general way (for example: "The couple plans a spring wedding") or may give the specific date and place of the wedding.

Photographs

Sometimes newspapers print the photograph of the prospective bride or couple, but it is a good idea to check with the local paper first. You may submit an 8½-by-10-inch glossy print with your name, address, and a request for return taped to the back of the photo. With luck, the picture will be returned or you may pick it up at the newspaper office. The statement "Miss Jennifer Lovejoy, whose engagement to Mr. Robert Baldwin is announced" should be attached to the photograph.

When Engagements Are Ended

Ending an engagement is always unpleasant, but the sooner this is faced squarely the better. Remember: No explanations are necessary!

If the bride breaks the engagement, she should return the ring to the groom, although it legally belongs to her. If the groom breaks the engagement, the bride may keep the ring if she likes. Any engagement or wedding gifts are, of course, returned immediately to family and friends.

An announcement in the newspaper is optional. Some people feel it is easier on everyone if a release is sent to the paper as follows:

> *Mr. and Mrs. Lloyd Jones of Franklin Village announce that the engagement of their daughter Maria has ended by mutual consent.*

Be sure, however, not to act hastily before submitting such a release. Lovers quarrel, but they also make up!

Joint Checking Accounts

In some cases, an engaged couple may wish to open a joint checking account or savings account to cover expenses for the wedding, reception, honeymoon, and so on. Be aware that complications can arise, as in the case of a broken engagement, when it is difficult to return gifts of money that have already been spent on deposits, household furnishings, and so forth. It is better to leave the money intact in the bank as long as possible.

Bridal Showers and Parties

The everlasting benefit when families meet each other at prewedding events is that both sides of the family and their friends become acquainted—possibly for the first time—and grow to know, understand, and hopefully like each other. Then, by the time the wedding day arrives, everyone feels more relaxed, and the reception is not a stiff, uptight affair; rather, it is filled with a lively spirit of warmth, congeniality, and friendliness.

Who Gives a Shower?

Any close friend, neighbor, relative, or member of the bridal party may offer to give a shower and mail out invitations. A member of the immediate family, such as a mother, sister, or grandmother, should not act as hostess—lest she be viewed as "grabby"—although family members may share the facilities of their home or give some financial aid.

Showers are usually given a month or more before the wedding. It is also a good idea for two or three people to plan a shower together rather than have many showers. It can become a financial drain on guests who are invited to more than one shower for the same person. One or two showers is a sensible limit, and each shower may be planned for a different group of guests. Fifteen people, more or less, is a reasonable number for a home shower.

Who Is Invited?

The hostess should consult with the bride (and the groom, too, if it is a couple's shower) regarding the guest list. Although only people invited to the wedding are usually invited to a shower, there may be exceptions, such as one's coworkers (who may decide to give a group gift), school friends, or members of a club. If such groups decide to give a shower, it is perfectly acceptable to limit the guest list to members of the specific group. Otherwise, the usual shower includes relatives and friends of the family, bridesmaids, and the maid or matron of honor. A couple's shower would also include the ushers, best man, and fathers of the bride and groom. (More about this later.)

Planning a Shower

The hostess and the bride select a date that is mutually convenient, and they decide what kind of shower is the most appealing—kitchen, linen, travel, or miscellaneous. The hostess may even hint to the guests on written invitations as to the couple's choice of décor—contemporary, provincial, crafty, Edwardian—along with color preferences. It is acceptable to mention on a shower invitation where the bride is registered, but it is never done on a wedding invitation. And yes, it is considered tacky to have a paper (money) shower, or a no-host luncheon.

The Bride's Responsibilities

As guest of honor, the bride should try to be considerate and help the hostess ahead of time in any way she can. She will arrive about half an hour early to offer help with last-minute preparations. She will assist by greeting guests and introducing them to one another. She will thank each person for his or her gift and write thank-you notes, especially to those people who sent gifts but were unable to attend the shower.

The Game Plan

A brief game or two always generates lively conversation, fun, and laughter. Any paper-and-pencil game, guessing game, or party game helps break the ice and allows people to get to know each other better. After the games, refreshments are served. The high point of the shower comes at the end, when the brightly wrapped gifts are opened and the names are read from the enclosed cards.

One of my favorite games, because it is a good mixer, is to pin the name of a prominent athlete, movie star, politician, or historical figure on the back of each guest. Then he or she walks around and asks people yes-or-no questions, such as "Am I living or dead? Am I an American?" In this way, each guest tries to figure out the name pinned to his or her own back.

The Couple's Shower

Several couples may enjoy splitting the cost and doubling the fun for a couple's shower for the bride and groom. Such showers and prewedding events are growing more and more popular in every community. Among the invited guests are the parents, bridesmaids, matron of honor, ushers, groomsmen, best man, and friends. Any type of party may be planned to suit the locale and the season, ranging from an informal cookout to a glamorous cocktail party, a charming brunch, or a beautiful buffet supper. An informal invitation reads as follows:

> *Janet and Bob Linney*
> *Mary and Bill Smith*
> *invite you to attend a shower*
> *in honor of*
> *Jennifer Lovejoy and Bob Baldwin*
> *Sunday, May tenth at five o'clock*
> *510 Oakwood Avenue*
>
> *RSVP   Kitchen Shower*
> *347-6443*

Be sure to give the last names of all persons involved, as it can be puzzling and difficult to link first names to the people you know through school, church, or work. It is especially important to give full names when friends of the bride and groom are invited by hosts whom they have never met!

Suggested shower themes for couple's showers include a kitchen/bar shower, a tool/garden shower, or a travel shower.

A Bridesmaids Party

The bride may wish to give a party in honor of her bridesmaids and matron of honor prior to the wedding. Mothers of the bride and groom are included and perhaps the flower girl and her mother. This is a grand opportunity to give the attendants their special gifts. The attendants, in turn, may also present the bride with a special gift at this time. It is best to let the bridesmaids know ahead of time if such a party is being planned, because the attendants may inadvertently plan a competing surprise party.

The Bachelor Party

The groom, his father, the best man, or the ushers may sponsor the bachelor party. Plans pertaining to the stag affair are usually kept secret (and the events grossly exaggerated). The bachelor party is a good opportunity for the groom to give his attendants their gifts. The traditional toast to the bride may start or close the festivities.

The bachelor party should be held several days before the wedding so it will not interfere with the rehearsal dinner. In some cases, bridesmaids and bachelor parties are scheduled for the same day, and the two groups join afterward. In general, bachelor parties are not held as often as in the past. Ushers often come from far away and frequently arrive just in time for the rehearsal on the day before the wedding.

Dear Edith,
We are having a rehearsal dinner for our son's wedding. There will be forty guests for a sit-down buffet dinner at round tables for eight. Do you think we need place cards?

ANSWER: It is thoughtful and convenient to have place cards, as it eliminates guests' confusion over where to sit. It also gives you the opportunity to mix people from both families so they may become better acquainted, or to seat people next to each other who have not been together for a long time.

Start by numbering an envelope for each table, say one to five. Each envelope will hold eight place cards. Write the names of the people you would like to have seated together on the outside of each envelope. Then, put the matching place cards in the envelopes until you are ready to place them on the tables. For example, table 1 may be made up of the bride, groom, some of their young relatives, and attendants. Table 2 may be made up of the bride's parents, the groom's parents, and out-of-town relatives. Table 3 may be made up of the clergyperson and spouse, grandparents, and possibly grandchildren or other relatives. Table 4 may be made up of a congenial group of young people, and table 5 may be made up of other out-of-town guests, relatives, a guest soloist, and so on.

The Rehearsal Dinner

It is becoming more and more popular for the wedding rehearsal to be held in the late afternoon, followed by a rehearsal dinner the evening before the wedding. Often, the groom's parents or relatives enjoy hosting this event because it draws them a little closer into the wedding circle. However, any close friend or relative of either family may opt for this honor.

Often, the rehearsal dinner is a jolly, informal, stand-up buffet with a relaxed and casual atmosphere. Or it may be a sit-down dinner with place cards at home, at a club, or at a restaurant. Guests at the rehearsal dinner include all members of the wedding party, both sets of parents, and the clergyperson or judge and spouse. The spouses or fiancé(e)s of members of the bridal party are also included. Unless there is something else planned for out-of-town guests (this is where in-town friends can help out), it is considerate to include them, too.

At this time, the bride and groom may choose to give the attendants their presents. This is also a good time to sign the marriage license, which is then given to the best man for safekeeping until just before the ceremony, at which time it is presented to the clergyperson or judge.

Place Cards

It is also possible, when there is a last-minute cancellation or addition, to be flexible and decrease a table of eight to a table of six or seven. Just remove the place setting and chair, since no one likes to sit next to an empty seat. It is also possible to easily increase a table of eight to a table of nine.

Family Receptions before or after the Wedding

Either set of parents may host a reception or dinner anytime before or after the wedding to introduce the bride and groom to friends and relatives. When the couple is being married far from the bride or groom's hometown, this is often the ideal solution. Such an invitation may read as follows:

Before the Wedding:

Mr. and Mrs. Lawrence Franklin
request the pleasure of your company
at a reception
in honor of
Miss Julie Franklin
and
Mr. Thomas Morris
on
Sunday, the sixteenth of May
from five to seven o'clock
Lord John's Inn
Highland Park, Illinois

Please respond
510 Liberty Street
Oak Park, Illinois 60011

After the Wedding:

Mr. and Mrs. Lawrence Franklin
request the pleasure of your company
at a dinner
in honor of the marriage of
Mr. and Mrs. Thomas Morris
on
Saturday, the fifteenth of May
at half past seven o'clock

124 Old Orchard Road
Rochester, New York

RSVP

A response card with stamped envelope is optional.

Parties for Out-of-Town Guests

It is thoughtful to offer a little extra hospitality when there are a number of out-of-town guests, especially when people come from a great distance. This is where friends of the family can be helpful. They may take the guests on sightseeing trips or entertain them at an informal gathering. A generous offer of this kind is always deeply appreciated, particularly the day before the wedding, when the bridal party is involved with the rehearsal dinner.

If the ceremony is scheduled late in the day, it is extremely considerate when a friend or relative offers to host a casual, light luncheon for the bridal party and out-of-town guests. The luncheon should be brief and informal, allowing guests to leave early to get ready for the wedding.

The Afterglow

A popular new trend is to entertain family and out-of-town wedding guests the day following the wedding. Sometimes this affair even includes the bride and groom! I had the pleasure of hosting a summer outdoor afterglow for my neighbor's daughter. Family and friends had flown in for the wedding from as far away as Denmark, and the afterglow in our garden was a perfect finale. People had a chance to relax, unwind, exchange stories, look at videotapes of the wedding, open more presents, exchange addresses, and say their fond good-byes before heading to the airport.

The party was scheduled from noon until three. I engaged a chef who brought his own equipment and prepared waffles for fifty people. He used two waffle irons and served crisp bacon and pork sausages with pitchers of melted butter and Michigan maple syrup. We also offered fresh strawberries, blueberries, and raspberries presented in large glass bowls. People helped themselves to a variety of beverages, including iced tea, coffee, wine, beer, and fruit juices. It was a good choice that helped settle our digestion after a night of merriment.

Before leaving, one of my Danish guests remarked, "This is a delightful new custom we are going to introduce in Denmark!"

Prewedding and Afterglow Party Suggestions

The more, the merrier; the fewer, the better fare.
PROVERB

Prewedding and afterglow party suggestions are listed below, beginning with a morning coffee or brunch, and continuing throughout the day and into the evening.

Morning Coffee—This is ideal anytime before noon. It could be either in a charming garden setting during the summer, using coordinated paper goods, or in a very posh setting in the winter, with a grate fire and your finest china. Beverages may be cold bloody marys, iced tea, or hot chocolate with whipped cream, along with sliced fresh fruit, coffee cake, or sweet rolls, served on trays with lace paper doilies.

Brunch—A poolside brunch on a sunny weekend may be as casual as a keg of beer or as elegant as bubbly champagne. An informal menu, indoors or out, between twelve and two o'clock usually consists of fruit, sweet rolls, and a casserole of scrambled eggs with bacon and/or sausage. A champagne brunch menu might include halved grapefruit, eggs Benedict or grilled fish with vegetables, dessert, and coffee.

Luncheon—A buffet luncheon may be served outdoors at home on a deck or patio. It may also take place indoors at a sit-down luncheon in a country club setting, or in the lovely private dining room of a restaurant with a view. The menu may be a glass of sherry, Dubonnet, or mimosa to precede the meal, followed by a chilled salad with dainty sandwiches, a glass of iced tea, and dessert. Optional is an ethnic Mexican, Greek, or Cajun meal including a hot dish, salad, dessert, and beverage. Another option is an Indian curried chicken, with rice and condiments, and a cold glass of beer.

High Tea—An afternoon tea is held in high esteem around the world, reaching all the way from England to Japan. A fashionable tea at home, after two o'clock and before five o'clock in the afternoon, for fifteen to twenty friends, can be as charming as a large, elegant tea for a hundred in a garden or country club. The menu always consists of a variety of sweets, dainty heart-shaped sandwiches, fresh fruits, mints, and nuts. Optional is a bowl of alcoholic punch. A tea dance with big band music returns periodically to popularity and is an amusing change of pace.

Champagne Tea—Along with the proper tea service, offer a champagne punch in a large silver punch bowl, which could be rented, along with the usual refreshments. A Silver Champagne Punch recipe consists of three magnums domestic champagne, one quart Courvoisier (brandy), and several dashes of bitters. Pour this over a ring of molded ice and serve it in a silver punch bowl. This makes fifty servings of three ounces each.

Cocktails—In any cozy setting, a theme cocktail party with light or heavy hors d'oeuvres is a delightful way to entertain, especially when you serve specialty drinks, such as mint juleps, margaritas, or nautical hot grogs, or a punch bowl filled with the typical English drink, whiskey sour.

Dessert Party—Taking place in the evening around seven or eight o'clock, the dessert party features an eye-pleasing menu consisting of a variety of tasty desserts: chocolate layer cake, almond torte, English trifle, fruit pie, or French pastries. For something a little unusual, cafe brulot, flaming crepes, or cherries jubilee add pizzazz to any gathering.

Dinners—Informal cookouts at home can be memorable with shish kebabs or grilled chicken, or a fabulous hearty soup served in a classic tureen with a fresh green salad and French bread, followed by ice cream with fresh fruit or berries. Or you may plan a sit-down dinner in the private dining room of a popular restaurant. To ensure the best service, choose from menus preplanned by the host. You may also preorder flowers for the table and prepare small bowls of mints and nuts, as well as place cards, to make the dinner appear more intimate and private. Because it is important to know exactly how many people will attend, it is wise to telephone anyone who has not responded to the written invitation. Mail does go astray and people do leave town, so there is no harm in a follow-up telephone call whenever necessary.

Notes

Chapter Three

Preparing for Marriage

Now everything is you
Everything that touches our lives
Touches us together
Like a violin bow
That begets from two strings, but one voice.

RAINER MARIA RILKE

When two people fall in love and decide to marry, the world and everybody in it seems perfect. All you need to do when you decide to get married by a clergyperson is to set the time and the place, right? Well, not exactly.

Premarital Counseling

Most clergymembers believe in getting to know the couple before they will agree to perform the ceremony. They have learned from experience that it is helpful to have one or more sessions with the bride and groom, during which questions can be asked and feelings expressed.

Premarital counseling helps you air your unspoken expectations. Friendly discussions may touch on lifestyle views, household responsibilities, extended family issues, friends, interests, sexuality, finances, and parenting. There may be a need to discuss an interfaith marriage or a second marriage.

Many couples who have had the privilege of marriage preparation have told me that these sessions have proven invaluable in helping them in their new relationship. They have found the clergy useful and not combative or judgmental, and the fresh point of view welcome.

The Catholic church, as well as some other major denominations, recommends a premarriage inventory that covers the most common areas of potential strain in married life, such as practicing the faith, sexuality, children, finances, and in-laws, and helps couples identify strengths and weaknesses in these areas. A series of questions is put to the bride and groom and is then sent to a computer center, where the responses are evaluated. If the couple is 70 percent or 80 percent compatible, then the discussion focuses on the 30 percent or 20 percent area of conflict—the goal being to

assist in possible growth there. A simple area of
difference, for example, may occur in the
practice of celebrating birthdays and holidays. What is the family tradition and custom
that each will bring to this marriage? Are there
conflicting feelings regarding these special occasions? Is a compromise necessary? Can you agree
on the compromise?

Clergy of various denominations may recommend one or more premarital counseling sessions,
each lasting about an hour, as preparation for marriage. These sessions may emphasize the seriousness
of the step being taken, accenting the role of true reli-
giosity in maintaining ideals and values, and offering further inspiration for
the future.

Here is an outline of a more-or-less typical routine for the average couple:

- Session One—The couple and the clergyperson or officiant become
  acquainted with each other. The goal is to relax and bring warmth and
  friendship into the relationship and to avoid any unnecessary tension.
  The officiant may ask how you first met, how long you have been together, what you do for a living, and where you will live. These are a few of
  the standard "getting to know you" questions usually asked.
- Session Two—(a) The marriage prospect and compatibility are evaluated.
  Is this a first or second marriage? What is the age of the couple? Has the
  couple addressed all the issues? Are there any children from a previous
  marriage? Literature for study is usually given out during this session, and
  stories are shared for everyone to laugh over and enjoy. (b) Continuation
  of discussions begun in previous sessions may be scheduled as the couple
  and clergyperson deem desirable. Further sessions may be scheduled by
  mutual agreement.
- Session Three—Discussion focuses on the specific examples and choices
  of marriage services, including special readings (secular or religious),
  music options, the participation of invited guests, and how the couple
  want to handle their vows.
- Session Four—The last meeting is usually a wrap-up session of wedding
  details where participants discuss printed programs, rehearsal, timing,

what the clergyperson will wear, seating arrangements of blended families, and the scheduling of the service.

Group Discussions and Seminars

In addition to the aforementioned counseling sessions with a clergy, there are other helpful programs available to the bride and groom. These are couple-to-couple counseling programs where an older couple reviews some of the considerations to be addressed before marriage. There are premarriage seminars such as Pre-Cana, which is a group discussion that may last one afternoon. Then there are weekends or an Engaged Encounter designed to give a couple an intense and honest look at their commitment to one another. Many Roman Catholic dioceses require that couples attend one of these programs prior to marriage.

Difficult Decisions

While thumbing through thousands of e-mail questions I have received from perplexed brides and grooms, I've noticed that many deal with the complicated situations that arise among stressed-out couples who are burdened by family pressures or whose parents are either divorced or too domineering.

Dear Edith,
My fiancé and I now live in Maryland, but we're thinking of getting married in my hometown church in Ohio. Do we have to get premarital counseling by the minister who marries us in Ohio?

ANSWER: Not at all! A minister of the same denomination may counsel you where you now live. This clergyperson will communicate with your minister in Ohio. If possible, the minister who will marry you will probably like to talk to you several days before the ceremony to go over your selections of the wedding vows. Otherwise, this may be done during the rehearsal.

What should the groom do if his mother refuses to attend the wedding because her ex-husband is invited? What should the bride do if Aunt Jane won't come unless her children are invited? Where should the biological parents of the adopted bride or groom be seated at the ceremony? How should the wedding invitation be worded when parents are divorced? How do you resist your family's pressure to have a two-year-old in the wedding party? How are divorced and remarried parents seated at the reception when they aren't on speaking terms? Who should walk the bride down the

Premarital interviews preferably take place as soon as possible, not just a week or two before the ceremony, so there would be time for a psychotherapist to help explore and resolve conflicts, or for delaying or even canceling the marriage.

I think the Catholics are on to something very good, and I wish [that members of the Jewish faith] had a more structured form of premarital counseling.

When there is a divorce, I often meet with the parents separately and tell them "I am not judging you," but that divorce causes pain to children, even though a divorce is sometimes necessary. The primary responsibility is not to add to the pain, but to act in whatever way one needs to in order to please one's son or daughter. I encourage a father, for the sake of his daughter's happiness, not to bring his live-in girlfriend to the wedding.

There are some Reform rabbis that officiate at mixed marriages under certain circumstances. I do not participate in mixed marriages, but I will officiate in a civil ceremony performed by a judge and offer a blessing. I will offer a private blessing to a couple under any circumstances, if the children are going to be raised Jewish.

I have been involved in more than a few second marriages, and they have worked out wonderfully. They turn out best when each partner in the second marriage is willing to assume responsibility for the failure in the first marriage.

Upon request, I will make some reference to a deceased parent to be with us in spirit, and I have no objection to a couple pledging brief personal vows during the exchange of rings.

—Samuel E. Karff, D.H.L., Senior Rabbi of Congregation Beth Israel, Houston, Texas aisle and who should give her away during a second marriage? How does one handle an interfaith marriage? How do you honor a deceased parent? Who tells the children from a previous marriage about the forthcoming wedding?

These and many other sticky questions are answered both in helpful premarital counseling sessions and in the following chapters of this book.

Young couples may be faced with difficult decisions when one set of parents is hosting a wedding on a modest budget, and the other parents want to invite everyone in town. In such a difficult situation, it is always best for the bride and groom to talk things over with their parents privately, and for all to maintain their dignity.

The same principle holds true when children from a previous marriage are involved. It is best for the parent to have a private, face-to-face conversation with the child to answer questions.

There are times when a bride or groom needs to be assertive and express herself or himself openly. As one bride said to her divorced parents, "It would make me very happy if, on my wedding day, you would sit together at the ceremony." When faced with a difficult decision, it is helpful to remember what Thomas Jefferson said: "In matters of principle, stand like a rock, in matters of taste, swim with the current."

Prenuptial Agreements

Originally, wealthy individuals used prenuptial agreements to protect their estates. Today, prenuptials are not only used for second marriages, to protect the children's inheritance, but also to protect both the bride's and groom's retirement benefits, IRAs, mutual funds, and property. More and more couples are employing this useful tool when contemplating marriage. Any prenuptial agreement should be reviewed by two lawyers (one for each person), signed by both parties and witnesses, and notarized.

Marriage Blessing

(Gregorian Tone V.S.)
(This poem was found in an old English church, located in the Highlands
on the border of Scotland, by Dr. William Donald of Mackinac Island.)

*Now the gates of happiness
open wide before thee;
And the path of love waits
smiling for thy feet.*

*God's sunlight crown all
thy days with gladness;
And his stars make every
evening glorious.*

*Love turn all thorns
into roses for thee;
And every cloud reveal
the splendor of heaven.*

*Prosperity deck thy hearth
with plenty;
And peace abide there
forever as thy guest.*

*Thy home be refuge
from every tempest;
A garden of cool springs
in summer's parching heat.
Thy children grow up strong
and beautiful around thee;*

*Every one in the image of God
our maker
May thy days be long
and of beauty;
And be thy strength
sufficient for thy tasks.*

*Love guard thee
within and within,
From this time forth,
forevermore, Amen.*

FRIAR TUCK

Notes

Notes

Chapter Four

The Wedding Budget and Calendar

Spend more imagination than money.

LYNDON B. JOHNSON

Fortunately, the success of a wedding does not depend on a limitless budget. Instead, it is careful, thoughtful planning that helps create the right atmosphere for a perfect wedding day.

Every couple must determine their own priorities. Since the guest list is the item that runs up the cost of the wedding more than any other, you must balance the guest list with the type of wedding you wish to have. For example, a daytime wedding followed by a stand-up reception is far less costly than a candlelight wedding followed by a sit-down dinner. A disc jockey instead of a band helps to bring down the costs, as does serving punch instead of having an open bar.

To compromise a bit here and there may be better than to lunge into a nightmare of impractical plans that must be scrapped—or worse, assumed as burdensome debts later. As the sayings go: "It's best to cut the cloth to fit the suit" and "Don't try to have a champagne wedding on a beer budget."

There was a time when wedding expenses were clearly defined and everyone knew his or her responsibility. Parents of the young bride hosted the wedding and paid all the bills, the groom or his parents paid for the honeymoon, and so on. Today, these lines are blurred, because families are more flexible. More often than not, the groom's parents may volunteer to make a contribution toward the wedding expenses or to host the wedding. More couples today are hosting their own weddings. In some cases, the bride's parents may clearly state the amount they are willing to spend, and the bride, the groom, or his parents may pick up anything beyond this sum. Whatever the final decision, it should meet with everyone's approval.

If the groom comes from a very social family that expects a large and formal wedding, and the bride comes from a family of modest means, the type of wedding must be discussed openly and agreed upon mutually. The bride and groom should sit down alone first and come to an agreement. Then the bride should talk to her family, and the groom should talk to his family.

If the groom's family expects a larger wedding than the bride's family can afford, the groom must explain the situation frankly to his family and ask them if they are interested in making a contribution. If, on the other hand, the bride's family prefers to host a more modest wedding, that is their privilege, and it should offend no one.

A good time to discuss the budget is when the invitation list is put together, if not before. The wording on invitations and announcements often depends on who is hosting the wedding or who is paying the bills.

For example, if the parents of the bride are giving the wedding, then the invitations are sent out in their names:

> *Mr. and Mrs. Loren Jay Lovejoy*
> *request the honour of your presence*
> *at the marriage of their daughter*

If, on the other hand, a couple host their own wedding, the invitation may read:

> *You are cordially invited*
> *to the marriage of*
> *Miss Jennifer Anne Lovejoy*
> *and*
> *Mr. Robert William Baldwin*

Please refer to Chapter Seven for further wording on invitations and announcements.

A Breakdown of Wedding Expenses

With today's unpredictable economy, it is difficult to give prices in anything but general terms. A good rule of thumb for a small, informal wedding today (about 20 to 30 people) is that it may run under two thousand dollars. The cost of a moderate or small semiformal wedding (about 125 people) averages somewhere between ten thousand and eighteen thousand dollars. The cost of a large, formal wedding is unlimited. Figuring in terms of percentages, wedding costs for 100 guests are as follows: 5 percent stationery; 10 percent photography; 25 percent clothing and gifts; 10 percent ceremony; 40 percent reception, including flowers and music; 10 percent miscellaneous. When there are more guests, the reception percentages rise and the other percentages drop accordingly.

These monetary figures can be sliced when friends offer innovations that help set a wedding apart. For example, one couple borrowed an antique car for the ride from the church to the reception—no limousine fee! Another couple accepted a relative's offer to have the reception in her garden—no rental hall expense! And then there was the bride who accepted a friend's offer to design her wedding gown—a big saving!

A word of caution: Never depend solely on a friend for free photographs. This important subject is discussed in greater detail in Chapter Twelve.

Wedding Obligations and Expenses

For your convenience, a summary of items that fall under the wedding budget is listed on the following pages in the traditional division of wedding expenses and responsibilities. Each family's circumstances are different, and this will affect your final decision.

Dear Edith,
I would like to ask a friend to sing at our wedding, but I am not sure if he expects to be paid. What should I do?

ANSWER: If your friend sings professionally at weddings and other occasions, you must approach him or her by first saying that you'd like to have him or her sing at your wedding, and then tactfully asking what the fee might be. It is up to your friend to give you a price. He or she might offer to give you a gift of song as a wedding present. On the other hand, if you ask a member of the family or a close friend to sing, you might merely tell him or her you'd be honored if he or she would sing at your wedding. Then you can reciprocate by giving the singer a memento of the occasion.

The Bride and Her Family

- Engagement party and photograph (optional)
- Bride's wedding dress and accessories
- Bride's presents for her attendants
- Bride's honeymoon trousseau
- Groom's wedding ring, if it is a double-ring ceremony
- Suitable gift from bride to groom (optional)
- Printed invitations (announcements optional)
- Formal wedding photographs, videos, and/or candid pictures
- Floral decorations at ceremony and reception, bridal bouquet, and flowers for bride's attendants
- Rental of awnings, tents, or carpets for aisle
- Fee for services performed by sexton, organist, or choir at church and music for reception
- Transportation from bride's home to church and reception
- All expenses of reception, including rental of hall or club, catering service, food, refreshments, including liquor*, wedding cake, and favors, if any
- Bride's doctor visit and blood test

* In some areas, and among certain ethnic groups, the groom traditionally provides the liquor or champagne for the reception. In other circumstances, the groom is expected to buy all the flowers for the wedding party.

The Groom and His Family

- Bride's engagement and wedding ring
- Engagement party (optional)
- Purchase or rental of wedding clothes for groom
- Return of rental clothes
- Groom's doctor visit and blood test
- Marriage license
- Clergyperson's fee or donation
- Gifts for the best man and ushers
- Suitable gift to the bride (optional)

- Boutonnieres for the groom and the ushers
- Bridal bouquet, when local custom requires it
- Bride's going-away corsage
- Corsages for members of both families, unless the bride chooses to include them in her florist's order
- Consult with fiancée and help arrange for lodging for out-of-town attendants and relatives
- Transportation after the reception
- Check that all legal, insurance, financial, and medical documents are in order
- Bachelor dinner (optional)
- Rehearsal dinner (optional)
- Honeymoon expenses

Bridesmaids' Expenses

- Purchase of bridesmaid's dress and all accessories
- Transportation to and from location of wedding (lodgings optional)
- An individual gift to the couple
- A shower or luncheon for the bride (may be shared)

Groomsmen's and Ushers' Expenses

- Formal attire or rental of wedding attire
- Transportation to and from wedding site (lodgings optional)
- An individual gift to the couple
- A bachelor dinner for the groom (optional) may be hosted by the groomsmen, the ushers, the best man, or the groom's father or relative.

Guests' Expenses

The groom's parents pay for their own transportation and lodging expenses, as do out-of-town guests. The parents of the bride and the groom may help in securing accommodations at the home of friends for bridesmaids and ushers, or may offer to pay any expenses that they wish to assume for out-of-town guests.

Clergyperson's Fee

It is always a puzzle to know how much to give the clergyperson for performing the wedding service. Most clergy do not have a set fee. There are times when they will perform a wedding for nothing, although I am told the average payment is fifty dollars. However, one might consider being more generous when a clergyperson spends several sessions counseling the bridal couple, guiding the rehearsal, and performing the wedding ceremony.

Other considerations include whether the wedding is to be held in a church or elsewhere. When the wedding is held in a place of worship, the clergyperson may have more responsibilities, such as checking with the custodian that the place is clean, heated, aired out, and so on, and that the bells are rung, if requested. In addition, when the reception is also held in the church after the ceremony, the clergyperson may have added responsibilities.

There is also the question of whether the couple are members of the congregation. If not, one might consider an additional amount as a courtesy.

When one compares the offering to the minister with the expense of say, the bridal bouquet or the wedding cake, it does put things into perspective.

The Professional Wedding Coordinator

Finally, a hint to the professional or working couple, who are living away from home: When you are pressed for time or not familiar with the community, or both, a professional wedding coordinator might be the perfect answer for you. Most large cities have wedding coordinators who are experienced advisors and take the place of the mother of the bride, who used to enjoy doing all the legwork and providing all the answers. With 60 percent of married women working, today's mother of the bride is either following her own career or is busy with other aspects of her life. The freelance wedding coordinator fills this gap. He or she has the necessary connections to help couples find that perfect place for the reception, select a caterer, choose the right music and florist, help with the wording of the invitations, and assist in making the arrangements at the church. The coordinator will cooperate with the minister, help guide the rehearsal ceremony, and even make arrangements for the honeymoon, if you like.

Hiring a wedding coordinator does not mean you give up control of your wedding. A good, experienced wedding coordinator will save you a lot of time and help you budget wisely. (Be sure to get references in order to avoid hiring someone who is learning the business at your expense!) He or she may work for an hourly rate or charge a percentage of the total wedding cost (usually 15 percent). The wedding coordinator brings repeat business to florists, photographers, caterers, and so on, which gives him or her a lot of clout, and this works to your advantage! Your wedding coordinator will handle the total wedding on your behalf, with your advice and consent, and will make sure everything runs smoothly.

You may find a wedding coordinator by word of mouth, in the yellow pages of your phone book, or by contacting the Association of Bridal Consultants, 200 Chesnutland Road, New Milford, CT 06776-2521, telephone 203-355-0464. They will suggest names of consultants in your area, whom you can interview.

The professional wedding coordinator is not to be confused with the wedding *consultant* you find in a department store, bridal shop, jewelry store, stationery store, or florist shop. Such in-house consultants are people who work in a store and specialize in helping the bride and groom with their gift selections, without charge.

Tipping

TIPS is an acronym for "To Insure Prompt Service." When the staff try their best to do a good job for you, they deserve a 15 to 20 percent tip. Tipping is a personal expression of gratitude for efficient service, and the following suggestions are merely guidelines.

The host of a reception may be asked to pay a deposit or an advance on a bill. Check whether gratuities are covered in the bill. If not, arrange to give a 15 to 20 percent tip to the caterer, the club, or hotel banquet manager at the end of the reception.

If gratuities are not covered, one may also wish to tip the maitre d' 15 to 20 percent of the bill, as well as the waiters, waitresses, and table captains. It is optional to tip bartenders, who may be tipped 10 percent of the total liquor bill, above the gratuities.

Powder room attendants may be tipped according to the number of guests, and the parking attendants may be tipped per car.

The host may also tip musicians, vocalists, and so on.

The Bride and Groom's Calendar

As Soon As Possible:

❑ Decide on the type of wedding and where it will be held, who will officiate, and how many guests will be invited.

❑ Discuss budget and estimate costs.

❑ Shop for engagement and wedding rings.

❑ Meet with your clergyperson. Set date and time of wedding.

❑ Compare and book facilities for rehearsal and wedding sites.

❑ Compare prices of local caterers, bakers, florists, musicians, and photographers. Check into party rental services for chairs, tents, glasses, and so on. Engage the services of these professionals as soon as possible.

Six Months before the Wedding:

❑ Choose attendants.

❑ Select wedding gown and attendants' gowns. Select groom's suit and attendants' suits. The couple helps mothers to blend gowns with each other and the rest of the party.

❑ Visit stores and compare furniture, appliances, and accessories. Register for gifts.

❑ Meet with insurance agent regarding insurance on ring, wedding gifts, and so on.

❑ Shop for invitations, announcements, and thank-you stationery.

❑ Check final invitation and announcement list with both families.

❑ Make hotel reservations and/or visit your travel agent regarding honeymoon trip. If necessary, arrange for passports. Check luggage required for honeymoon.

Two or Three Months before the Wedding:

❑ Get birth certificates. Get physical, blood test, and inoculations, if necessary.

❑ Address and stamp envelopes.

❑ Meet with musicians and go over music for ceremony and reception.

❑ Meet photographer and go over plans for ceremony and reception. Make appointment for black-and-white newspaper photo.

❑ Confirm flower orders. Decide on rose petals, confetti, rice bags, or birdseed, if permitted.

❑ Finalize arrangements for rehearsal dinner and reception site. Check menus with caterer.

❑ Order wedding cake. (Groom's cake, almond souvenirs, or truffles, and so on, optional.)

❑ Check with bridesmaids regarding gown, shoes, and so on. Collect measurements from ushers and order rental suits.

❑ Select gifts for attendants. (Monogramming optional.)

One Month or Six Weeks before the Wedding:

❑ Mail invitations.

❑ Arrange for transportation, maps, and lodging for out-of-town members of the wedding party.

❑ Attend prewedding parties. Give gifts to bridesmaids and groomsmen.

❑ Schedule final fitting of bride and groom's clothes. Break in shoes.

❑ Sit for wedding portraits and prepare newspaper announcement.

❑ Check on honeymoon tickets and hotel confirmation.

❑ Make hair appointments. Bride schedules makeup artist (optional).

❑ Decide where bride, groom, and attendants will dress before the wedding.

❑ Get marriage license when required.

❑ Move belongings to new home and arrange utilities, telephone, and mail. Put someone in charge of gifts at reception.

❑ Write thank-you notes.

❑ Spend some quiet times together.

One Week before the Wedding:

❑ Attend prewedding parties. (This is a good time to tell relatives and special friends where to sit during the wedding ceremony, unless you have arranged for pew cards.) Visit with out-of-town guests.

❑ Confirm number of wedding guests to caterer.

❑ Make final check with florist, photographer, musician, and baker.

❑ Check on final alterations of groomsmen's suits.

❑ Pack for honeymoon trip.

❑ Write thank-you notes and place cards.

❑ Spend a quiet evening with your family.

The Day before the Wedding:

❑ Pack toiletries. Lay out wedding clothes and going-away outfits. Make out check to clergyperson or judge.

❑ Go to beauty parlor today or tomorrow.

❑ Attend rehearsal and dinner, and go home early.

The Day of the Wedding:

❑ Eat a substantial breakfast.

❑ Get dressed for wedding. Attend the ceremony and reception, and have a wonderful time! Change into traveling outfit. Thank everyone sincerely. Leave for honeymoon.

After the Wedding Day:

❑ Have wedding announcements mailed (optional).

❑ Call home. Write postcards to members of the wedding party and family while on honeymoon (optional).

After the Honeymoon:

❑ Unpack and get settled. Exchange duplicate gifts. Write thank-you notes. Invite your first guests to dinner!

Notes

Notes

Chapter Five

Planning the Wedding and Honeymoon

Hear the mellow wedding bells
Golden bells!
What a world of happiness their harmony
foretells!
Through the balmy air of night
How they ring out their delight!

EDGAR ALLAN POE

Early Decisions

Early decisions that influence every detail of the wedding and the budget must be carefully considered.

- Will you have a religious or civil ceremony?
- Where will the ceremony and reception be held?
- What is the best time of day or year to have the wedding?
- How many guests will be invited? (Traditionally, the fact that the groom has been married before has no bearing on the size or elegance of a bride's first wedding.)

A Religious or Civil Ceremony Site

Selecting the clergymember, mayor, or judge goes hand in hand with choosing the site of the ceremony. If a priest, minister, or rabbi is selected, the wedding will probably be held in a church, temple, college chapel, rectory, or pastor's study. But if a mayor or judge is selected, the ceremony could take place at City Hall, the judge's chambers, or just about anywhere. Some rabbis, judges, and Protestant ministers will perform wedding ceremonies in a hotel, restaurant, private club, garden, or in the home of the bride's parents. Sometimes a friend or relative may offer his or her home or garden for the wedding. In some communities it is possible to rent a lovely mansion, art center, public park, or historic site for both the wedding and reception. Your library may have the helpful directory *Places* by Hannelore Hahn, a Tenth House Enterprises publication. This book lists ten cities with two thousand wedding site suggestions.

Wedding Sites

No matter where the ceremony takes place—in a church, club, hotel, garden, or home—the wedding site may be either in the bride's or the groom's hometown or in the city where the engaged couple currently live and work. When families are scattered all over the country, another option is to plan a destination wedding, which may be located in a popular vacation spot.

Almost any good-sized room can be transformed into a churchlike setting. Furniture may be moved or removed as the case may be; folding chairs can be set in a V formation, which makes it possible for people near the wall to see the altar; space may be left for a center aisle between the rows of chairs; and a raised platform may be installed for the ceremony.

Dear Edith,
My fiancé would like to be married in church, but I've always dreamed of a home wedding. How can we reach a fair decision?

ANSWER: Before reaching a conclusion regarding the place to be married, let's consider some other factors that may help you both.

1. How many people do you plan to invite? If it is a large group, a home may not accommodate everyone. If it is a small group, the guests may feel lost in a large church.

2. What about the budget? A church wedding may mean lower expenses. For a home wedding, it may be necessary to rent numerous items, including arches, standards, and even a tent.

3. What kind of reception are you considering? Some churches have a social room and even offer catering services, which is a convenience. Or, you can be married in church and have the reception at home.

4. When you have weighed the pros and cons of the total wedding arrangements, including the time of day, the number of people, the budget, and the type of reception, then you may be better able to come to a mutual agreement on the place for the ceremony.

A combination of ceremonies and reception sites may be considered, but let's limit ourselves first to a few popular sites for the ceremony.

Home Weddings

When the ceremony takes place indoors at home, it is not necessary to seat every guest during the ceremony. Home ceremonies are usually brief, and as long as there is seating for the older generation, the rest don't mind standing. Just be sure to remove tipsy tables and lamps, as well as small pieces of furniture, to prevent breakage.

Church or Synagogue Weddings

As one mother said to her daughter: "You may get married anywhere you want—as long as it's in a church!"

Aside from the established religious reasons for wanting to be married in a church or synagogue, there is the practical advantage. The building will accommodate a large number of people with little expense, and the ceremony may be followed by a simple reception in the reception hall or elsewhere.

Clubs, Halls, or Rented Sites

Any private setting in a club, restaurant, hotel, hall, or facility may be chosen for a large or small group of people. Here, charges may vary from a few hundred dollars to one thousand dollars or more.

Garden Weddings

Outdoor weddings are lovely, if you can depend on the weather. But always have an alternate plan in case of rain. If the budget allows, a good alternative is to rent a tent.

Tents

The advantage of renting tents is twofold: They create a colorful, festive atmosphere at home, and they offer complete protection for guests against hot summer sun or drenching rains.

When the wedding ceremony is held at home, a tent may be rented for the ceremony with either full or partial seating accommodations, with a platform area used for the altar. The platform later may be converted into a dance floor.

Guests may return to the house and go through the receiving line after the ceremony. Meanwhile, a quick changeover is taking place outside. The tent that was originally used for the wedding ceremony is turned into a dining tent. Tables that were concealed behind shrubs or in a nearby garage are brought in and set up. Chairs that moments before were used at the ceremony are placed around the tables. By the time guests have gone through the receiving line and enjoyed their first drink, everyone is ready for the reception.

For a more elaborate arrangement, two tents may be set up, one for the ceremony and one for the dinner.

Tents come in all sizes, from sixteen by sixteen feet, which will seat twenty-five guests, to up to sixty by ninety feet, which will seat more than five hundred guests. There are also tents that will accommodate as many as five thousand guests. They can be heated and, in some areas, air-conditioned.

Tents may be color-coordinated with the wedding scheme. They come in a variety of stripes—red/white, yellow/white, green/white, solid pink or blue, or transparent crystal. The inside of the tent may be decorated by a florist with greenery and lights.

The tent is usually set up a couple of days in advance, which helps keep the ground dry under the structure. A tent may be placed in the back or front of a house or over an asphalt driveway or patio. It may even be erected over a swimming pool, to provide a focal point for outdoor dancing.

Companies providing tents are highly specialized, and large tenting companies will supply many states.

Exceptional Wedding Sites

There are times when traditional wedding sites—church, home, country club, summer place, or hotel—do not meet the need. There could be many good reasons. For example, the home is too small; one is not affiliated with a church or country club; the summer place is off-season or too remote; a hotel is too expensive, or the date is already booked. In some cases, a couple prefers to *get away* and opt for utter privacy.

There are places in the United States that specialize in streamlined weddings, either on land or sea. They have people in charge who make it easy for the bride and groom to solemnly seal their vows. They have a variety of information at their fingertips, and they can do it on short notice.

Most of us have heard of such popular wedding sites as the Coco Palms Resort in Kauai, Hawaii; King's Chapel in Williamsburg, Virginia; the Martha Mary Chapel in Dearborn, Michigan; the Little Brown Church in Vale, IA; and last but not least, Las Vegas or Disney World.

Shipboard Weddings

Shipboard weddings on cruise boats have doubled in recent years and are often considered bargains. A nondenominational minister or civil officiant usually performs marriages aboard ship. The cruise line's wedding planners will advise you on the fees, licensing, and documentation necessary. Foreign marriages are recognized in the United States as long as the requirements of the foreign government as well as those of your home state are met. To arrange for a shipboard wedding, contact your travel agent or cruise line.

Picturesque Wedding Sites

Recently, I had the pleasure of attending two unusual and picturesque weddings. One wedding took place on sparkling Emerald Bay in Lake Tahoe, California; the other took place on historic Mackinac Island in Northern Michigan.

The situation is unique in Lake Tahoe because California and Nevada have a law pertaining to silent marriages. This law states that men and women over eighteen who have been living together for some time are considered married. If you wish to avoid any notices of your marriage being posted in the newspaper, it is possible to formalize your marriage in Lake Tahoe without waiting and without blood tests. The Confidential Marriage License is issued by the Eldorado County Clerk in California and by the Douglas County/Lake Tahoe Clerk in Nevada.

Many couples take advantage of this loophole and plan to both marry and honeymoon in this scenic area, where all the professional services of wedding consultants, chapels, reception sites, florists, bakers, photographers, musicians, limousines, beauty salons, and so on are available. For a full-color *Wedding Service Guide,* write to Lake Tahoe Weddings and Honeymoons, Lake Tahoe Visitors Authority, 1156 Ski Run Boulevard, South Lake Tahoe, CA 96150.

One of the local service businesses helped organize the morning wedding I attended. It was able to provide a minister, who would do a religious, traditional or civil service, as well as recommend a photographer and florist, and offer the choice of an indoor or outdoor wedding site. For this intimate wedding, a dramatic and breathtaking outdoor site was chosen, located one thousand feet above shimmering Emerald Bay. During the brief ceremony, guests stood on smooth, flat boulders beside a small, gurgling waterfall, while the shade-offering ancient white pine trees reached up to the sunny sky!

After the ceremony, the reception was held at the nearby Christiania Inn, which provided pink tablecloths, fresh flowers, and a delicious buffet meal with champagne, wedding cake, and a dance floor.

Admittedly, weddings on the weekends are scheduled every hour on the hour, but they are handled well with a professional flair.

Weddings on historic Mackinac Island in Northern Michigan are also unique. There are no automobiles on the island, only horse-drawn carriages and bicycles! Of the hundreds of weddings that were held on the island last year, 75 percent of the couples say they wanted to get married there because they saw the movie *Somewhere in Time.*

If you write to the Mackinac Island Chamber of Commerce at P.O. Box 451, Mackinac Island, MI 49720, the Chamber will mail you, free of charge, its *Wedding Guide,* which contains all the information you need to plan the destination wedding of your dreams. Whether you plan to send out 1,500 invitations and rent a whole hotel for the weekend, or to have an intimate twosome with a glass of champagne in a white horse-drawn carriage, you will find all the professionals you need listed in the Mackinac Island Wedding Guide. You have a choice of wedding coordinators to help with all the details involved in planning a long-distance wedding, and there are good professional photographers, bakers, and florists on hand. You also have a choice of disc jockey or live music. Shepler's Mackinac Island Ferry provides free passage for the bride, groom, and clergy; provides discounted fares for your attendants, family, and friends; and offers cruises for receptions and rehearsal dinners.

There are three scenic churches from which to choose a wedding site, including Saint Anne's Catholic Church, which dates back to 1695. In addition, there is a Butterfly House, a Gazebo, a powerboat named *The Czechered Frog*, and Victorian hotels that may be used as the location for a picturesque wedding. Clergy and officiants to perform the ceremony are available, if needed.

I attended an unusual secret wedding on Mackinac Island for a couple from Marquette, Michigan. They had just completed building a new home and invited all their relatives and friends to an open house the day *after* their island wedding! When the guests arrived at the open house, they were surprised to learn that their hosts were newlyweds, and that the housewarming presents they had brought were, in truth, wedding presents. The family and friends enjoyed the party and the delicious wedding cake, and they applauded the videotape of the previous day's wedding—romantic carriage ride and all!

Venice and Other Foreign Places

Who could decline an invitation to attend a wedding in Venice? Naturally, on the way to the wedding, I went by gondola past the Grand Canal to an ancient palazzo where the ceremony and reception were being held. I ascended a wide double staircase to a high-ceilinged room lit with candles hanging from huge chandeliers. The effect of the candles, which cast a flickering glow on all the invited guests, was spectacular! Although beautiful, I also know that planning for this wedding was challenging.

When planning a wedding in a foreign country, be sure to check the requirements of the country you will visit, as well as any other countries in which you may travel. When traveling to any foreign country except Canada, Mexico, and some Caribbean nations, you will need a passport, which may take a month to process. In lieu of a passport, Mexico and some Caribbean countries require only a photo ID—usually a driver's license—or other proof of U.S. citizenship, such as a voter registration card.

Passports and Travel Documents

A passport cannot be obtained in one's married name before the wedding. Traveler's checks, international airline tickets, and visas should be issued in one's premarriage name. Hotel reservations and domestic airline tickets may be reserved in one's married name. It is best to carry a duplicate copy of your marriage license with you, just in case you are challenged. In some countries, a couple traveling together must have proof of marriage.

Travelers need immunization against diseases when leaving North America, Hawaii, the Caribbean, or Europe. Your doctor should have this information. If not, contact Travel Health Services, 50 East 69th St., New York, NY 10021, telephone 212-734-3000.

Every country has different civil and religious laws pertaining to marriage. My friends found that getting a marriage license in Venice, Italy, was too complicated, so they were secretly married in the United States before they left. Of course, the guests who attended the wedding were not made aware of this stratagy.

Theme Weddings
Ethnic Wedding Themes

Couples often like to accent their country of origin during their wedding. Following are a few suggestions for creatively incorporating your heritage into your wedding:

- The bride and/or groom may wear a gown or suit in honor of his or her heritage. (A bride might wear a Japanese kimono or an Indian Sari, and a groom might wear a Scottish kilt.)
- Songs may be sung or music played during the ceremony and/or reception (Irish tunes, German Lieder, Italian Opera).
- Short poems or readings in a foreign language may be introduced during the ceremony. This may also be done in honor of a deceased loved one.
- The wedding color scheme can be planned around national colors, using flags in centerpieces or ribbons in bouquets.

Seasonal and Other Wedding Themes

Some couples may enjoy having a wedding that incorporates the season or another favorite theme. Below are just a few wedding theme ideas:

- A Victorian high tea wedding might be accented with fans, gloves, lace, and parasols. Place a tiny gazebo on top of the wedding cake, and play waltz music.
- A nautical theme may be achieved with blue-and-white decorations, using seashells and rope for accents in the centerpiece. Serve a seafood buffet at the reception.
- A Hawaiian luau might include flower leis for the guests and bright flower centerpieces accented with shells and floral prints. Ukulele players or recorded Hawaiian music could accompany hula dancers. Serve a punch made with tropical fruit juices in coconut shells.
- A Renaissance wedding reminiscent of *Romeo and Juliet* could include brocade gowns, plumed hats, and large pieces of jewelry. The music might feature mandolin, lyre, or harpsichord. Serve spiced wines and propose toasts with a Shakespearean touch.
- For a Valentine's Day wedding, mail heart-shaped invitations. Trim the bride's bouquet with red ribbons and lace. Select bridesmaids' dresses in red velvet or rose chiffon. Serve a heart-shaped wedding cake. Feature a strolling cupid singing love songs.
- For a Christmastime wedding, the bride could carry a fur muff, and her attendants' dresses could be trimmed in red or green velvet. Festive music and caroling would be appropriate at the reception, and the centerpieces could be accented with holly, poinsettias, and pine cones with silver or gold bows.

For more theme ideas, two excellent books are *Pick A Party* by Patty Sachs (Meadowbrook Press, 1997) and *Storybook Weddings* by Robin Kring (Meadowbrook Press, 1999).

Setting the Date

When setting the date for the wedding, several factors must be considered, including the season, the day, and the time.

Naturally, couples leaning toward garden weddings—at least in the

North—know winter is out of the question. Similarly, couples yearning for candlelight ceremonies will not choose summer. Lent is usually not chosen by Christians, at least not for a religious ceremony, though simple marriages with or without a clergyperson do take place during these forty days of penitence. Christians rarely choose Sunday for a wedding, nor do religious Jews marry on the Sabbath (Friday sundown to Saturday sundown) or on the High Holy Days.

One should bear in mind that the time of day and the day of the week will determine the number of acceptances and regrets. Both afternoon and evening weddings followed by a reception held on Saturday or Sunday are much better attended than those held during the week. During vacation periods and holidays, many people have family conflicts and are unable to attend weddings, unless they are notified in advance. (See Chapter Seven.) For most people, Saturday is the favorite day because it is convenient for guests to attend.

The Time of Day

Many weddings take place in the afternoon and are followed by a reception. Evening weddings with candlelight services are usually more formal and are followed by either a reception or a dinner and dancing. Popular times of the day vary throughout the country.

The Guest List

The guest list can be as unmanageable as a puppy and can grow just as fast!

When a couple are paying for their own wedding, the guest list will probably include a large percentage of the couple's mutual friends, with a sprinkling of close relatives.

Coworkers and Acquaintances

The question is sometimes asked if all one's coworkers must be invited to a wedding; if their spouses must be invited; and if one can put a blanket invitation up on the bulletin board for everyone to read.

The answers, generally speaking, are as follows: In a large office, if one has exchanged hospitality with one or two coworkers, one may send an invitation to those people at home, addressed to the individuals and their spouses. You should not put a "come one, come all" invitation on the bulletin board for everyone to see. It's okay to invite your boss to the wedding. In a small office it is best to follow the "invite no one or everyone" rule. The final answer in most cases is the obvious rule of courtesy and good manners, which is neither to single anyone out, nor to hurt anyone's feelings. Tempting as it is, it is best not to talk much about the wedding at work.

Finally, one needn't feel obliged to invite coworkers to a wedding unless that is what one chooses. Remember that when a coworker is requested to attend a wedding, his or her spouse probably won't know anyone, and he or she will also feel obligated to buy a present.

When Parents Host the Wedding

When parents are paying for the wedding, the guest list can turn into a stumbling block if not handled tactfully from the beginning. It is only natural that parents wish to include many of their close friends, because sharing the pleasure doubles the fun! This group ought to be limited, nevertheless, to people who have known the bride and groom and who are interested in their future. It ought not to include all the parents' friends and acquaintances, as this is not a party to pay off social obligations.

On the other hand, in many ethnic circles it is customary and expected for parents to open the wedding celebration to the whole community, with festivities lasting for several days.

In checking over the guest list with their parents, the bride and groom may not be in complete accord with them, but ought to compromise if possible. For example, they may not be aware of the genuine interest that their parents' friends have shown over the years, because they were too young to remember. Fortunately, the final decisions always rest with the bride and groom.

When both sets of parents live in the community where the wedding will take place, the guest list is equally divided into thirds—one-third for the bride's parents, one-third for the groom's parents, and one-third for friends of the bride and groom. When one family lives far away, the in-town family usually invites more people than the out-of-town family. If there is any confusion or conflict, the best way to clear it up to everyone's satisfaction is to have both families meet and discuss the guest list informally.

It is becoming more common for the groom's parents to offer to share in the expense of the wedding and/or reception, particularly if their guest list is long. However, their support should not be expected. And if the bride's family choose to host a modest wedding and reject a kind offer from the groom's family, it is their privilege to do so. In such a case, if it is not possible for the families to meet, the bride may write as tactfully as she can to the groom's parents and advise them as to how many guests can be invited altogether. She should ask for a copy of the groom's parents' limited list as soon as possible and hope they will understand that the number of guests is restricted for various good reasons.

Is it necessary to invite all the relatives? Not really. If there has been little or no communication in years and the relatives live far away, there is no need to invite them. Still, it is friendly to send an announcement of the marriage, which does not require a gift in return.

Children at the Ceremony and Reception

Some people like to bring small children to church weddings, and it can be a thrilling and memorable experience for these little folks. However, infants are uncontrollable and unpredictable, and they may start to cry at the most tender moment of the ceremony. It is not always possible to depend on word of mouth to get the message across that infants should remain at home. Therefore, the farsighted bride and groom might arrange for infants to be taken to a nursery, which many churches provide, or they may instruct the ushers to seat parents with infants in the last row or on the aisle, so they can make a quiet getaway if necessary.

If a formal sit-down dinner is planned after the wedding, it may be necessary to restrict the number of children attending the reception to those in the wedding party, especially if this is a large family with dozens of cousins, nieces, and nephews. It can be done if youngsters are limited to those over a certain age, with no exceptions. Close friends and relatives can help spread the word, or you may state on the invitation: "Dinner for Adults Following the Ceremony."

When children are welcome, some couples plan to entertain and feed their little guests. They may provide a babysitter or a costumed character appropriate to the season, such as the Easter Bunny or Santa Claus. One thoughtful bride provided a space to be checked on the response card stating "Children's Meal." She then provided pizza for the little folks at a separate children's table.

Special Guests

Special guests may include people who have been employed in the home, such as babysitters, housekeepers, caretakers, and others who are devoted to the family. It is nice to invite a special teacher, a friend's older brother, or anyone who has touched your life in a special way. Also, if you have a warm feeling toward someone who lives far away, send an invitation to him or her. He or she will be thrilled to share your happy news, even if attending your wedding is impossible.

You may wish to invite your bridesmaids' and ushers' parents if you know them well, but this is optional.

Persons with Handicaps

If anyone in the wedding party or among the guests uses a wheelchair, remember to consider this when selecting a site. Arrangements can be made for a portable ramp at the entranceway. Ramps may be rented from a truck rental firm. Bathroom facilities should be checked as well.

Security Guard

The question has been raised as to how to prevent someone undesirable from crashing a wedding. If this is a concern, hiring a security guard might be advisable. A security guard can also keep an eye on wedding gifts if necessary.

Cancellations

Much as everyone loves weddings, unforeseen circumstances can arise that will prevent some people from attending, so be sure to take this into consideration. The number of wedding guests will grow smaller as the day approaches because of these unfortunate last-minute cancellations. Some estimate the number can reach 25 percent, although 15 percent is more usual. It is important to estimate carefully how many people will actually attend, because this affects the cost. The caterer or person in charge of handling the reception is experienced in allowing for last-minute regrets; however, he or she must be advised by a certain date, or the host will be billed for every guest, present or not.

Sending Invitations in Waves

People have been telling me recently that some couples compile an "A list" and a "B list" for their invitations. As regrets come in from the A list, invitations are mailed to people on the B list. This risky method *might* work if people on the A list and B list are not friends or neighbors and won't be comparing notes. But if word gets out that your invitations have been sent, the people on the B list might feel like second-class citizens when their invitations arrive two weeks late. Therefore, I still feel that the traditional rule of sending out all wedding invitations on the same day to everyone is the kindest and most courteous way to go.

The Final Guest List

The final list of names will be compiled from both sides of the family and from the bride's and groom's list of friends. After checking for duplications and making sure that no one has been overlooked, you are ready to order your invitations and announcements.

Computer Files and File Cards

A time-saving plan is to take the final guest list and transfer it to your computer or onto file cards. List the name, address, and phone number of each guest and indicate acceptances or regrets. Also, note any gifts received for shower or wedding, and indicate whether gifts have been acknowledged. Both the bride and groom will find this filing system handy for future reference.

The Honeymoon

Some couples plan a weekend honeymoon, some plan a month-long honeymoon, and some plan a delayed honeymoon. For the latter, it may be more practical to settle into the new apartment or home immediately after the wedding and delay the honeymoon until a mutually convenient time.

If you are planning to take off on a long wedding trip, it is wise to secretly book a room in a nearby hotel on your wedding night. You will probably be too disoriented and exhausted to enjoy taking off for anywhere. It is far better to get a leisurely start the next day.

The honeymoon location should be considered very carefully. It should be an area that the bride and groom will enjoy equally. For this reason, some have suggested that what this country needs is an ocean in the mountains! When considering a honeymoon site, talk to people who have been there and whose tastes you share. Don't be afraid to ask a lot of questions about where to stay, what the place has to offer, where to eat, and what to wear depending on the time of year. It is good to know that you never need a raincoat in California during the summer months, but that you always need a sweater in the summer in the northern half of the United States.

Make a point of finding out in advance what kinds of things there are to do after you arrive and what they cost. Are there free concerts in the park? Free museum tours? Public beaches? Art fairs? State fairs? Free industrial tours? Good public transportation? If your lodgings are centrally located, you may save money on transportation. The money you save can then go toward the price of your room. Check with the local newspaper or magazine and write to the Chamber of Commerce or Visitors and Convention Bureau. Also, it pays to shop around with more than one travel agency.

If one of you gets seasick, don't choose a cruise! Or, if one of you is fair-skinned, avoid tropical sunshine. Decide whether both of you prefer to spend your honeymoon in isolated surroundings, with only good books and tapes for entertainment, or if you would like to land in the middle of a major city with elegant restaurants, theaters, and shops. Or is camping by a trout stream in the mountains or sailing on blue waters your idea of heaven?

Your travel agent will be happy to give you brochures and help you get your hotel and airline reservations confirmed in writing. Agents are aware of special packages for honeymooners, including weekend deals in hotels. Always tell hotel management that you are on your honeymoon; they may send you champagne or upgrade your room. Be sure to allow enough time to arrive promptly at the airport, train depot, or cruise ship.

Finally, a honeymoon doesn't have to be a twosome the whole time. Don't be surprised if one person chooses to read while the other person opts to take a walk. It is also possible to make friends while you are on your honeymoon. It is up to you to ask people to join you for a meal or share a sightseeing trip. Sometimes lifelong friends are made this way.

When you return from your honeymoon, rested and eager to settle in your new home, you will want to invite your friends and relatives for coffee and tell them about your trip. It's a delightful way to begin your new social life together.

Notes

Notes

Chapter Six

Planning the Reception

Music I heard with you was more than music
And bread I broke with you was more than bread.

MUSIC I HEARD WITH YOU

Since reception expenses cover such a large percentage of the total budget, I shall discuss planning for the refreshments, rentals, and so on in detail now. In another chapter I will discuss what takes place during the reception (who stands in the receiving line, how to cut the cake, and so on).

Few people have an unlimited budget at their disposal; therefore, it takes a bit of juggling to decide early on what is important to you and what is not. Since everyone invited to the wedding should be invited to the reception, now is the time to settle on the size and place. You'll want to ensure that there will be sufficient funds in reserve to cover the additional wedding expenses for music, flowers, gifts, photographs, and so on.

When There Is No Reception

There are times, at small church weddings, when there is no reception. The bride and groom, along with their attendants and family, may greet their guests informally in the vestibule of the church or any pleasant spot near the exit. The wedding party may adjourn later to share a meal.

Reception at Church or Synagogue

Many churches and synagogues have a social room, for which a small fee is charged, available for wedding receptions after the ceremony. Most churches do not allow any wine or alcoholic beverages to be served, although they may be served in synagogues. Some congregations provide all accessories, such as tablecloths, silver, and china, and they may even suggest the name of a caterer. At a church, the menu usually consists of a nonalcoholic punch and soft drinks, with small sandwiches and cake. If the church or synagogue has a lawn or a garden, the doors may be opened (weather permitting) and the guests may stroll outside. Piano or guitar players are bound to add gaiety and sparkle to the occasion.

Private Reception

The reception may be held immediately after the ceremony in a home, restaurant, or club. The bride's parents' home is a favorite and traditional setting for a wedding reception. Refreshments may be served indoors at a stand-up buffet table, or if space allows, at casual seating. During warm weather, if the club room or house is too small to seat all the guests, a tent may be set up outdoors in the garden, and the indoor facilities may be used for a coatroom, bathroom, dressing room for attendants, and kitchen.

Remember that at a brief reception it is not necessary to provide chairs for everyone, because it is pleasant for guests to walk about and mingle. Usually some chairs and tables are provided for older friends and relatives. When there is dancing, rented cafe chairs and tables are functional.

Informal Home Reception

In some cases, friends and relatives may offer to prepare refreshments, help serve, and clean up. Decide in advance what you are going to serve and when it will be served and select platters, bowls, china, flatware, napkins, glasses, serving utensils, flower holders, and candlesticks. Tape a small label to each bowl or platter indicating the intended contents—fruit, cheese, sandwiches, and so on—and place the appropriate serving utensil on each platter and in each bowl. You can even make a diagram of the buffet table in advance. Most communities have party rental stores where much of the above-mentioned equipment may be rented. Renting tableware gives the buffet table an important, attractive, uniform appearance, instead of looking like a casual picnic or potluck supper.

To be sure that everything will go smoothly on the big day, designate someone to be in charge of the kitchen, someone to see that platters are kept filled and remain appetizing in appearance, and someone to pour champagne, serve punch, or handle the bar. Remember, the bride and groom and family will be much too busy having pictures taken, talking to guests, and cutting the wedding cake to supervise the refreshment table.

Buffet versus Seated Meal

I am frequently asked, "Should we serve a buffet or sit-down meal?" Many people have very definite ideas on this subject, while others are undecided. The answer is that both ways are correct, and the decision is a purely personal preference.

Buffet Service—The facts to be considered here are as follows: If you choose to have a buffet, or self-service, plan to have more than one guest line, so that guests do not have to stand in a long line. Experienced hosts set up the buffet starting with plates at both sides of the buffet table, forming two lines. For a larger group, set up two buffet tables, side by side, and have four lines.

The buffet table is always set in a logical sequence. The dinner plates come first, followed by the hot food (precut meat, vegetables, potatoes, and casseroles), and then the cold food (salads, ring molds, bread, and rolls). Flatware is at the end of the buffet; it is handier for guests to pick up the flatware rolled in a napkin after they have helped themselves to the food.

Semibuffet—You may also consider serving semibuffet or full-service buffet, in which case the tables are set with tablecloths, flatware, and glassware, and the waitpersons serve the liquids, clear the tables, and serve the dessert.

Coffee served with dessert may be poured from a coffee urn from a side table holding cups and saucers. Do not set the table with coffee cups, because that gives the undesirable effect of a coffee shop, rather than a fine dinner setting.

Plate or Banquet Service and Russian Service—For a more elegant, formal wedding reception, one may either have a plate or banquet service, in which food is precut and garnished in the kitchen on individual plates and brought to the guests. Then there is the most formal service, called Russian service (a holdover from the days of the czars), during which the food is precut in the kitchen and attractively arranged and garnished on serving platters. The platters are offered to each guest from the left. A skilled waiter with an assistant serves each guest, or the guest may serve himself or herself from the platter. Russian service requires trained, uniformed staff and spacious seating.

Seating and Spacing

Round tables that seat eight are preferred because they are more congenial. However, long tables will accommodate more people in the same amount of space.

Allow ten square feet for every sixty-inch round table that seats eight people and allow twelve square feet for every seventy-two-inch round table that seats ten people. This guideline provides adequate room for chairs and for serving by waitstaff.

A thirty-by-ninety-six-inch rectangular table seats ten people comfortably, and a thirty-by-seventy-two-inch rectangular table seats eight people comfortably.

If it becomes necessary at the last minute to subtract or add one or two people, it may be done easily if you plan well from the start. Seat eight people at each table for eight and ten people at each table for ten; then you may add a guest without extreme crowding or subtract a guest without creating a big gap.

Here are some spacing examples: A forty-square-foot tent accommodates sixteen round tables to seat 128 people. An eighteen-square-foot dance floor will accommodate thirty-eight couples if you allow three square feet per couple.

Service

Caterers tell me there is little cost difference between serving buffet style or plate service. More food is required for a buffet, because you want every last guest to enjoy the spectacle of an attractive buffet table rather than a picked-over, skimpy table. Plate service requires more staff to adequately serve guests.

If a properly trained waitstaff is available, then opt for plate service; otherwise, semibuffet service is preferred.

What do we mean by proper service? For example, guests at every round table should be served each course simultaneously by the waitperson, so guests can begin eating together without having to wait too long for others to be served. Also, each table should be cleared at the same time and not until the last guest has finished eating. Dessert should not be served until the entire table has been cleared, and waitpersons should not hopscotch from one table to the next.

In conclusion, when making your final decision, various factors should be weighed: the setting (indoor or outdoor), the space, the informality or tone of the reception, the age of the guests, the equipment and abilities of the caterer and staff, and the budget.

Diagonal Stripe Napkin Fold

The Diagonal Stripe is an ideal place for a favor, souvenir menu, name card, or flower.

1. Fold into one-quarter size. Leave open at upper right.

2. Turn down one upper-right corner two inches.

3. Fold over corner twice for diagonal across napkin.

4. Turn down next upper right corner. Tuck into diagonal to same width.

5. Overlap top and bottom under napkin.

6. Place vertically on table, with souvenir, name card, or flower tucked in diagonal fold.

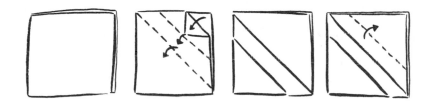

Party Rental Stores

Party rental stores have mushroomed all over the country. People depend more and more on this convenient equipment-rental service, especially for home or garden weddings.

Most party rental stores supply anything from one dozen glasses to tables, chairs, bars and tents, and many include table linens, lace skirting for the buffet and cake tables, flatware, chinaware, and glassware, as well as platters, chafing dishes, pitchers, and bowls. They also carry floral standards and arches for garden weddings, along with portable dance floors and champagne fountains. The latter come with full instructions.

Some party rental stores have several grades of linen, including damask, silver-plated table service, and a varied selection of wineglasses, while others offer only cotton cloths and stainless-steel flatware. As always, it pays to shop around.

To save time and energy, telephone the rental store ahead and ask a few pertinent questions, or have them send you a brochure of available items. Most rental stores pride themselves on giving good service, because word-of-mouth referral is what keeps them in business. Orders will be delivered in cartons at a predesignated time, and the order must be repacked in cartons ready for pickup.

To assure first-choice selections, rental supplies must be reserved early, as many other people will be booking their orders well in advance.

The Wedding Cake

The highlight of every reception is the charming ritual when the bride cuts the first slice of cake, which she offers to the groom to signify that she is willing, now and forever, to share her life with him. Included in almost every wedding album is a photograph of the bride and groom performing this symbolic bit of domestic life.

Selecting the right wedding cake involves looking at samples of cakes and comparing prices. Most bakers have pictures and order forms that include all the necessary information describing the cake, the delivery date and time, the address of the reception site, the name of the person who will receive the cake, and the bride or groom's name and phone number in case there are any questions. The terms of payment will be included, as well as the amount of the deposit. The baker will keep a copy and give one to the couple for reference.

If the bride and/or groom have the talent and inclination, he or she may undertake baking the wedding cake for a small wedding. Or perhaps a talented friend, relative, or neighbor has the know-how and experience.

One advantage of selecting a cake from a professional baker is that he or she has the ability to transport a large

Q&A

Dear Edith,

We have chosen a very beautiful wedding cake and would like to know if we can freeze the top to be enjoyed on our first anniversary. Some people tell me it won't keep well in the freezer for a year.

ANSWER: Commercial cakes (such as Sara Lee or Pepperidge Farm) sold in grocery stores are made to keep in the freezer for a year. Homemade cakes or those ordered from a bakery will only keep up to three months; then they become dry, and the icing may crack or weep.

It is much wiser to enjoy the cake upon return from your honeymoon or on your one-month anniversary. Or you may opt to use the top of the cake as a centerpiece on your first anniversary. In this case, it should be kept in a box that is wrapped in foil and plastic, or in a large poultry freezer bag.

You may also have the bakery make only the top of your wedding cake out of fruitcake. This does keep a very long time and may be eaten on your first anniversary.

cake and assemble it at the reception site, and—in case anything happens to the cake—has a backup crew to come to the rescue. A disadvantage is that a bakery cake is more expensive.

How big should the cake be? The measurements for a wedding cake depend on the size of each round, which is then assembled into numerous tiers. For example, in a three-tiered cake, a six-inch round provides approximately 14 servings, a ten-inch round provides approximately 39 servings, and a sixteen-inch round provides approximately 100 servings. Altogether, this three-tiered cake provides 153 average-sized servings. Many caterers are more generous with their portions, however.

Wedding cakes can be any shape—round, heart-shaped, square, or graduated in tiers. For a military wedding, the cake may be baked in the shape of the bride or groom's corps insignia. (Cutting the cake is described in Chapter Sixteen.)

What flavor? Any flavor—vanilla, carrot, lemon, or chocolate—with any kind of filling may be used. For a very large cake, however, a pound cake holds up best.

When selecting the decoration for a wedding cake, all white or white with a touch of pastel is usually the prettiest and most appetizing. A natural look is favored, with leaves tinted green and rosebuds tinted pink or yellow. A beautiful smooth coating known as rolled fondant, which is made of powdered sugar dough, may cover the entire cake or may be shaped into bows, drapery, and flowers.

Fresh flowers and leaves are also very popular for decorations. The buffet table on which the cake is placed may accent the colors used on the cake, which in turn ought to blend with the reception's color scheme.

Besides floral decorations, romantic symbols like swans, bells, doves, hearts, or cupids are frequently used to decorate cakes, but it is not usual to put writing on the cake.

Whether the cake is made at home or in a bakery, top ornaments are very similar. A small nosegay of fresh flowers, such as lilies of the valley, baby orchids, or stephanotis, can be inserted in a small vial of water at the top of the cake. This keeps the flowers fresh all through the reception. Or it is easy to make orange roses by using a sharp knife to cut orange peel in long spirals from a large orange. The strips are rolled up, orange side out, and fastened with a small pick to the cake. These are placed on the cake at the last minute, just before the guests arrive. The orange roses are garnished with sprigs of fresh mint or any small green leaf.

The Groom's Cake

Originally, the groom's cake was referred to as the wedding cake, and what we think of today as the wedding cake was called the bride's cake.

The groom's cake is usually a dark fruitcake and is sometimes served by the groom at the rehearsal dinner. It may also be given as a souvenir to the guests at the reception, in which case it is packed in a small white or silver box, tied with a ribbon, and placed at each person's place at the table. At a buffet, the boxes are stacked on a tray near the door, and every guest takes one home as a memento. The boxes may be printed with the name of the couple and the date. Those who are superstitious will put the groom's cake under their pillows that night to dream of the person they will marry.

A popular alternative to the groom's cake is a souvenir gift of chocolate truffles, packaged two to a box and tied with a gold ribbon.

Getting It All in Writing

When the reception is held in a church, hotel, restaurant, or country club, make sure that the person in charge of arrangements puts it all in writing for you! Too often, the person making all those lavish promises is no longer around come the day of your wedding, and you are left with a person who chooses not to honor the agreement—or worse, surprises you with hidden charges. When you have all the arrangements written clearly on official stationery with a signature, there can be no doubts! The following is a brief list of items you must have in writing:

The Date and Hours

Luncheons are usually served between 12:00 and 2:00 P.M., but your guests may choose to linger. Tea receptions are held between 2:00 and 5:00 P.M., and cocktail receptions between 5:00 and 7:30 P.M. A dinner is served between 7:00 and 10:00 P.M., and this celebration may last until the wee hours, or until the band stops playing. Usually one has a light menu at an earlier hour of the day and a heavier menu for a later hour.

Be sure you know when the room will be available for decorating and when you have to be out of there. I've known people whose reception was going full swing when they were unexpectedly asked to leave because the room was reserved for another group!

The Service

Find out exactly how many people will be available to do what. If you expect top-quality service for a sit-down dinner, there ought to be one waitperson for every eight guests. Ask about valet parking, coatroom checking, bar staffing, and cleaning charges.

The Food

Know what food will be provided and how it will be served. Will platters and chafing dishes be stainless steel, copper, or silver plate? Will platters be garnished? Will paper doilies be used?

The Liquor

Check on the corkage charge. There are various ways this can be figured. One way is to charge per person, which strikes a balance between those who drink and those who do not. The advantage of this system is that no one needs to count bottles at the end of the evening. Some caterers charge per bottle, and you are charged for all opened and empty bottles. You can choose the type of liquor you wish to have served—house brand, call brand, or premium brand. The bottle price should include the fee for the bartender, mixes, and glassware. Least popular, because it is time consuming, is to charge per drink at the bar.

What time will the bar be opened and closed? What kinds of glasses are available for champagne, beer, wine, and punch? Will there be wine bottles on the dinner tables, or will it be poured by waiters? Will after-dinner drinks be served?

The Tables

What kind of tablecloths and napkins are available? Will they be in good repair and neatly pressed? For a sit-down dinner, will there be sufficient flatware—knives, forks, and so on—for each course? Will each table be cleared before dessert is served? Will coffee be served with the dessert? (Again, request that coffee cups be placed on a side table to avoid looking like a coffee shop.)

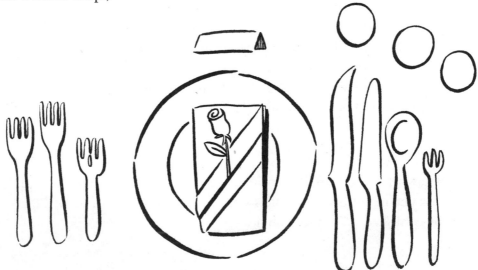

The Price

Is the price quoted per person, and does it include tax and tip? Are there any hidden charges? Some places charge extra when you bring your own wedding cake: There is a service charge for cutting and serving the cake.

Selecting the Right Room

The first consideration is the size of a room in relation to the number of guests. If the room is too large, people will feel lost in it and won't have much fun. If the room is too small—hot, noisy, and crowded—people will feel equally uncomfortable.

For a daytime reception, select a room with a lovely view or with windows through which the sun shines. For an after-dark reception, select a room that has sparkle, one with mirrors or crystal chandeliers. Have the draperies drawn shut, and check to be sure they blend with your color scheme.

Sometimes a room that looks undesirable in bright daylight can be camouflaged with soft candlelight and flowers and end up looking most attractive in the evening. Or a room that is plain can be decorated with rented plants that look colorful and charming. You can create magic with lighting and flowers!

For sit-down lunches or dinners, check whether the room has easy access to the kitchen—to be assured prompt service for hot meals. When you have an orchestra, check for platforms, microphones, and musical outlets.

Finally, know the fire laws regarding the use of candles and flammable materials. (You may need to clear this with the fire department, which will sometimes station a firefighter to stand by on special occasions.) Fire codes usually limit the number of persons a room can legally hold.

Caterers

How does one go about finding a caterer? The best way, of course, is to sample their wares. Some caterers primarily serve industry events, such as banquets, meetings, and conferences, while others specialize in private functions, such as weddings, anniversaries, engagements, and confirmations. Some caterers do both.

There are also all types of caterers. You could have someone who is a fine cook and will prepare and serve a dinner for sixteen or sixty in your own kitchen, or someone who will partially prepare some dishes at his or her home and then bring them to your reception. You could also call a large professional catering service with mobile kitchens, which will wholly or partially prepare and serve a meal. Some caterers supply everything, including fine linens, china, and crystal, while others supply only the food and personnel.

An experienced, professional caterer will welcome your suggestions and help develop your reception so that it reflects your own taste and personality. He or she may use your own recipes, if you wish, and keep them confidential; supply you with bonded, trained waitstaff and bartenders; and free you from all responsibilities before, during, and after the party.

A professional caterer will ask for a party-planning conference and confirm all arrangements either in duplicate or triplicate. A conference with a caterer or party consultant should be as honest and aboveboard as any conference between you and your clergyperson. Trust your caterer's judgment, which is based on years of experience. Tell him or her exactly what your budget is, what your facilities are, and how many people you plan to invite, and he or she will tell you if your wishes are possible and how they can best be realized.

It is a good idea to have a run-through when planning a large party at home. Some hosts don't realize until the last minute that their kitchen facilities are inadequate, that a borrowed pan is too big for their stove, that their electrical wiring is inadequate for all the extra cooking equipment, and so on. Be sure you test the working order of any stored, infrequently used articles, such as a fifty-cup coffeemaker or folding tables. Then, when the day of the wedding arrives, there won't be any last-minute emergencies. Instead, everything will be just perfect!

Alcoholic and Nonalcoholic Beverages

Since the greatest cost of a reception involves the choice of beverages, I shall go over this subject carefully, item by item. Nonalcoholic beverages, hot or cold, are the least expensive. Served with style, a punch in a crystal or silver punch bowl is a favorite at church receptions where no alcohol is permitted. When possible, it is thoughtful to offer both alcoholic and nonalcoholic beverages to your guests. A smooth way to limit consumption of alcohol without offense is to serve guests a few drinks and allow them to visit awhile. When it is time for the cake to be cut, fill the champagne glasses for the last time so that everyone may toast the bride. After the bride cuts the first piece of cake, have staff serve each guest a slice along with a cup of coffee. While the guests' attention is thus diverted, no one notices that the bar is being dismantled.

Nonalcoholic Punch Recipe

There are many excellent punch recipes available. I suggest this party punch because it is not too sweet and it complements a heavily iced wedding cake. Whenever I have served it, people have begged me for the recipe. Youngsters and adults alike enjoy it.

2 cups boiling water
4 tablespoons black tea leaves
3 large lemons
2 cups sugar
4 cups cold water

1 teaspoon vanilla extract
1 teaspoon almond extract
2 bottles (28 ounces each) ginger ale, chilled
1 can pineapple chunks, frozen

Pour boiling water over tea leaves. (Not tea bags—loose tea leaves taste better than tea bags and are less expensive.) Cover and steep for 10 minutes. Wash lemons, extract juice, and keep the rinds. Combine sugar, water, lemon juice, and rinds and heat in a medium-sized pan, stirring until sugar is thoroughly dissolved. Strain tea through sieve and add to hot lemon-sugar mixture. When cool, and not before, stir in vanilla and almond extract. Chill until serving time. (The tea extract may be prepared days in advance and kept in a gallon jug.) At serving time, pour tea mixture into punch bowl and add chilled ginger ale. Float frozen pineapple chunks in punch. No ice required. Makes 30 cups. (Recipe reprinted by permission of Hawaiian Visitors Bureau.)

You could also serve chilled bubbling grape juice that looks and sparkles like champagne in either punch or champagne glasses. Or you could serve hot coffee and tea at a tea table. There may be a single or double tea service, one at each end of the table, depending on the number of guests. Designate a guest of honor to sit and pour at one end of the table, and designate another person to replenish the teapot and coffeepot during the reception.

Alcoholic Punch Recipe

A mixed drink, such as a whiskey sour or a bloody mary, or a light punch can be mixed and served from a punch bowl or poured from a pitcher. Far less expensive than an open bar, a delicious wine punch is frequently the perfect answer for an indoor or outdoor reception.

For a summer wedding, try the recipe below:

FRESH PEACH PUNCH

¼ cup sugar
¼ cup brandy
3 pounds fresh peaches, sliced

1 fifth red wine, chilled
1 fifth white wine, chilled
1 bottle domestic champagne, chilled

Add sugar and brandy to peaches and let stand 3 to 4 hours. Just before serving, place in crystal punch bowl and pour red and white wine over peaches. Add block of ice, and at the very last minute add champagne. Makes 24 servings.

Beer

Serving beer has become more and more popular at all kinds of receptions, especially among the young set. Consider serving some fine imported European beers, as well as some of the increasingly popular domestic micro-brews, to add some variety. If you do decide to serve beer, do not condone drinking from bottles or cans, as the beverage tastes better served in a glass. It is also important to remember that when taking pictures at a reception, a can or bottle of beer in plain view detracts from what otherwise might have been a memorable photograph. Instruct the bartender to immediately dispose of unsightly empty bottles. For more informal occasions you may use a keg, but never serve canned beer. Almost any kind of glass may be used nowadays for serving beer. You may even serve beer in a fluted champagne glass, which conserves the bubbles. Or you may pour beer into a wineglass, as one would serve a fine wine. Only fill the glass two-thirds full, as you do with wine—not to the rim. As with all beers, pour boldly to create a foamy head. The ideal temperature of beer is about fifty degrees Fahrenheit.

Champagne

Here's to champagne the drink divine
That makes us forget all our troubles;
It's made of two dollars worth of wine
And six dollars worth of bubbles.

Champagne served from a bottle, punch bowl, or champagne fountain is very elegant. The price varies according to the country of origin. Imported French champagne is considered the finest. However, there are many excellent domestic champagnes on the market.

The Open Bar

It takes a great variety of liquor to stock an open bar. Fortunately, most liquor store owners will accept returns of unopened bottles. A brand of scotch, bourbon or rye, gin, rum, vermouth, vodka, and blended whiskey usually suffice. Sherry, Merlot, and white wine are also frequently called for, as well as soft drinks. Mixes, such as soda, Perrier water, quinine water, and ginger ale are needed, as well as lemons, limes, cherries, olives, and cocktail onions. Buckets of cubed and/or crushed ice complete the list. You may instruct the bartender in advance when you want the bar to open and close. He or she will inform the guests with a last call.

Tray Service

There are times when it is preferable to have the waitstaff pass trays of prepared or mixed drinks. In this case, the choices are usually limited. Some drinks are mixed ahead and kept chilled in the refrigerator. When ready to serve, ice and garnishes are added.

How Many Bottles?

No matter how often one entertains, there is always the question of how many bottles of liquor are needed. The average guest will have two or three drinks; or figure roughly one drink every half-hour per person. In gauging how much champagne is required, a good rule of thumb is to figure one bottle for every two people. For a large group and a long reception, it's better to use small six- or eight-ounce glasses, because people frequently set a glass down and forget where they put it. For this reason, for a long reception with dancing and so forth, plan on using about three glasses per person. You can judge the number of bottles needed using the following guide:

1 case of liquor = 12 bottles

⅕ bottle = ⅕ gallon or 7 ounces less than a quart

⅕ bottle liquor, using 1-ounce pony = 25 drinks

⅕ bottle liquor, using 1½-ounce jigger = 18 drinks. (The difference between a pony and a jigger is ½ ounce.)

⅕ bottle champagne, using 3-ounce glasses = 7 drinks

Step Savers

When setting up an improvised bar indoors or out, drape a cloth that reaches all the way to the floor around the edge of a large, sturdy table or aluminum folding table. Behind this cloth you can store extra liquor, lemons, limes, glasses, soda, empty bottles, and a wastebasket. Keep a large tray handy for used glasses.

Planning the Entire Menu

When planning a menu for any occasion, it has been my experience that the easiest way to spark ideas is to jot down food categories on a sheet of paper. For instance, when planning the menu for a reception, the main food categories are cheese and eggs, fish, fowl, meat, vegetables, fruit, and sweets. By the time you have selected one item from each category, you are already off to a solid menu-planning start. Within each category, consider additional subcategories, such as hot and cold, sweet and sour, or soft or crunchy. For example, it is not a good idea to offer a salad with vinegar dressing when serving wine. And finally, it is important to think of the color in the food itself, such as orange carrots, red beets, black olives, or green melons. If one needs additional color, this may be achieved with garnishing, such as green parsley, watercress, mint leaves, sliced cucumbers, red tomatoes, watermelon, radishes, or cabbage leaves.

Here are some menu suggestions that may be helpful when planning a wedding reception, brunch, luncheon, buffet, or sit-down dinner. No

Hardy-Grober Wedding Menu
Walloon Lake Country Club
Saturday, July 16, 1999

Hors d'oeuvres
Smoked whitefish pâté in baked phyllo cups, garnished with golden caviar
Sun-dried tomato and wild leek pâté, garnished with bell pepper triangles
Veal and walnut country pâté, garnished with whole-grain mustard
and sliced cornichons

Soup
Stafford's Chilled Black Cherry

Hemingway Salad
Crisp romaine, beefsteak tomato, smoked pheasant,
and freshly grated parmesan, tossed with garlic vinaigrette
and sprinkled with cornbread croutons

Breast of Chicken Voyageur
Boneless chicken breast stuffed with dried cherries, pecans, wild rice,
and accompanied by a sage cream sauce

Vegetables Walloon
Asparagus/carrot timbale garnished with fresh herbs

Hiawatha Whole Grain Rolls

Wines
Moreau Chardonnay 1983 — Venegazzu 1980 — Champagne Freixenet

Trillium Wedding Cake
Mocha fudge chocolate cake with raspberry liqueur filling
and buttercream frosting

Café Noir

doubt your final decision will depend on the number of people invited; the season of the year (always taking advantage of fresh fruits and vegetables); the location, if near water where fresh fish or crabmeat is plentiful; the budget, where your imagination counts; and the amount of volunteer or professional help that is available.

The setting for the menu on the preceding page was Northern Michigan, where French Voyageurs once traveled, Hiawatha once lived, and Ernest Hemingway spent his summers as a youth. A hand-painted souvenir menu on parchment paper was rolled up, tied with a ribbon, and given to each guest.

Menu Ideas for a Traditional Daytime Reception

The minimal requirement for a wedding reception is a beverage, a finger food, and a wedding cake. A beverage may be a choice of either an alcoholic drink or a chilled punch, sparkling grape juice, or hot tea and coffee. Other beverage options are:

- Champagne by the glass
- Champagne punch with fresh strawberries or peaches (in the summer)
- Champagne fountain
- Hot punches or grogs (in the winter)
- Wine punch or wine by the glass
- Cocktails and mixed drinks

Refreshments: Canapés and Finger Sandwiches

Most caterers figure eight pieces of finger food per person. This could mean six tiny sandwiches or canapés and two sweets per person.

Most people enjoy preparing a wedding reception menu that is a little fancier in appearance than, say, the traditional cocktail party menu. Finger sandwiches may be either open-faced or closed. They may be cut into small rounds, triangles, hearts, squares, and oblong shapes using a wide variety of breads, such as white, whole wheat, rye, and black.

A variety of spreads may be used in the sandwiches or as fillings in miniature puffs, cherry tomatoes, or mushrooms. Some popular mixtures are made of minced turkey or chicken, ham or tongue, chopped olives, salmon, or anchovies. Open-faced sandwiches may be garnished with a slice of black or green olive, a sprig of parsley, a strip of red pimento, a miniature pickle, or a slice of hard-boiled egg.

In addition, you may wish to serve rolled watercress, cucumber, or asparagus sandwiches, as well as some canapés, such as pinwheels made of bologna or ham and cream cheese.

Hot hors d'oeuvres may be passed as well, such as bite-sized portions of quiche, bacon wrapped around water chestnuts or pimiento-stuffed olives, caramelized bacon, hot toasted mushroom sandwiches, hot chutney cheese rounds, or cheese puffs made with phyllo dough and filled with feta cheese, called by their Greek name, tiropites. Stuffed eggs seasoned with curry or chutney are always in high demand, and so are assorted cheese trays, or lovely vegetable or fresh fruit baskets.

Along with the wedding cake, a fancy sweet table may be set with three-tiered stands on which miniature French pastries, nuts, and mints are displayed.

Wedding Brunches

These may be served buffet style, or guests may be seated at long or round tables. The beverage served may be wine, champagne, or sparkling grape juice, with a choice of bloody marys or screwdrivers. A tray of stuffed mushrooms, cubes of cheese, or cheese sticks may be offered with the beverage.

Buffet Style

For cold buffet brunches, luncheons, or suppers, a forks-only type menu is most convenient, and one buffet table or several tables, referred to as stations, are popular. A variety of molded salads may be displayed on the buffet table, such as a tomato or avocado aspic, a chicken or ham salad, a herring or shrimp salad, a curried potato salad, or a marinated vegetable platter. A variety of croissants, rolls, or English muffins may be offered with a choice of jams and jellies. The wedding cake is served for dessert at a separate table, and chocolate mints may be offered as well. Hot coffee or tea completes the menu, although in some cases iced tea with mint leaves or iced coffee may be preferred.

A Seated Wedding Brunch

When guests are seated, a glass of fruit juice, a fresh fruit cup, or half a grapefruit may be waiting at each place setting. The second course may be eggs Benedict on toast or English muffins served with Canadian bacon, fresh melon balls, or a spiced peach or apple. Miniature pecan rolls or Danish pastries, as well as wedding cake, may be offered along with a beverage.

A Wedding Luncheon

While guests go through the receiving line, champagne may be offered. Hot and cold hors d'oeuvres may also be passed to the guests or served from a buffet table, where the guests may help themselves.

Suggested Menus
Seated Luncheon

Menu One

First Course:	Hot bouillon or cream soup, seafood cocktail or salad, or chilled melon balls
Second Course:	Chicken or seafood crepes, quiche, or Monte Cristo sandwiches
Dessert:	Chocolate truffles Wedding cake Tea and coffee

Menu Two

First Course:	Fresh fruit cup
Second Course:	Boned breast of chicken with country ham
	Mushroom sauce
	Rice balls
Third Course:	Asparagus and shrimp salad
Dessert:	Individual ice-cream molds
	Petit fours
	Wedding cake
	Tea and coffee

Summer Buffet Supper

Poached cold salmon with dill sauce
Platters of cold sliced turkey and roast beef
Condiments
Fresh zucchini-vegetable casserole
Thin party breads
Fruits, melons, and berries
Macaroons
Wedding cake
Tea and coffee

Seated Formal Dinner

First Course:	Seafood cocktail or mock turtle soup
Second Course:	Filet of beef tenderloin with béarnaise sauce
	Lattice potatoes
	Hot creamed spinach with coconut
	Cloverleaf rolls
Third Course:	Hearts of artichoke salad
Dessert:	Miniature fruit tarts
	Wedding cake
	Tea and coffee

Notes

Chapter Seven

Stationery

"The horror of that moment," the king went on,
"I shall never never forget!"
"You will, though," the queen said,
"if you don't make a memorandum of it."

ALICE IN WONDERLAND
LEWIS CARROLL

The Guest List

The best advice I can give you is to make a memorandum of everything in connection with a wedding—especially when it comes to the guest list!

Everyone on the guest list, including the parents of the groom, all members of the wedding party, and the clergymember or judge and spouse, should be sent invitations through the mail. These will be treasured by all as happy mementos of your wedding day. You may wish to mail one to yourselves, too, because not only will it be fun to receive your own invitation in the mail, it will also let you check how long it takes to be delivered.

Addressing Invitations

When sending a wedding invitation to a married couple, it is courteous to address it to both husband and wife, even if you know only one member of the couple through work or school, or if you assume that only one person will be able to attend.

Envelopes should be addressed by hand or with a fine-script font from your computer; labels are never used. If you need help addressing invitations, ask a friend, relative, or bridesmaid with a fine hand to assist, or hire a professional calligrapher.

Duplicate Master Guest List

When compiling a master guest list from both families, ask that names be spelled out completely with full addresses and zip codes, just as they will appear on the envelopes. For instance, an entry on the list should read "Mr. and Mrs. John Roger Gallagher," not "Mr. and Mrs. J. R. Gallagher."

Then, when it is time to address envelopes, the job will go much faster.

It is also helpful both now—and later at the reception—if a duplicate guest list is distributed to each set of parents. Knowing all the guests' names and where they are from will help parents make friendly conversation with the new people they meet.

Friends of Guests

You are not obligated to invite escorts for your single friends, but if you would like a single person to bring a friend, insert a note reading "Please bring a friend." Better yet, if you know the friend's name, write at the bottom of the invitation in matching ink, "Please bring Mr. Jonathan Belding." Then send the friend an invitation as well. An engaged man or woman may ask to bring his or her fiancé(e), and a personal invitation should be sent to that person. When the words "and Guest" are used, they should appear on the inner envelope.

There are times when space does not permit singles to bring guests. In this case, it is considerate either to arrange for them to be picked up by a mutual friend, or to assign someone to introduce singles to other guests and seat them at a friendly table with other singles at the reception.

Invitations, Announcements, Informals

Once the wedding list is complete and the date and hour of the wedding are set, it's time to concentrate on the wording and style of the invitation.

There are three basic types of wedding stationery to consider: (1) the invitation asking guests to the ceremony and/or reception; (2) the announcements informing friends and relatives that the wedding has taken place; and (3) the informal to be used for thank-you notes, handwritten invitations, or brief messages.

The Informal Home Wedding

For a very small, informal wedding (possibly planned on short notice), the bride may telephone or write personal invitations on good stationery, stating the time and place of the wedding. For example:

> April 9, 2000
>
> Dear Aunt Mary,
>
> John and I will be married on Saturday, May 1, at two o'clock in my parents' home. We are so eager to have you with us to share our happiness! Please let us know if you can come.
>
> With love,
> Susan

Telephone number optional
Return address on note and envelope

Or the parents of the bride may send a handwritten note:

> July 12, 2000
>
> Dear Catherine,
>
> Jennifer and Bob will be married Saturday, August 9, at five o'clock in the Presbyterian Church. We would like you and Jim to come to the ceremony. There will be a small reception afterward in our condominium, and we look forward to your being with us.
>
> Fondly,
> Diane

Telephone number optional
Return address on note and envelope

Original Artwork

Some couples, particularly professional artists, like to design their own wedding invitations. If sufficient time is allowed to complete the job, to address the envelopes, and to mail the invitations four to six weeks before the wedding, then designing original invitations can add that personal touch that is so important to every wedding.

Recently I have been asked about printing wedding invitations on a computer. If it is done tastefully on a good grade of paper, with matching envelope, there is no reason why you shouldn't design your own wedding invitation on the computer. Be aware, though, that inkjet printing on an outer envelope may smear and become illegible if it gets wet. Laser printing is your best bet.

Calligraphy

Calligraphy is the beautiful art of writing by hand, sometimes used in addressing envelopes and designing invitations. There are many styles of calligraphy from which to choose. For wedding invitations or announcements, usually only one copy is handwritten, and the original is then taken to a printer to be copied on heavy paper in quantity. For small weddings, each invitation may be written by hand.

Mr. and Mrs. William Smith
510 Liberty Street
Oak Park, Illinois 60011

MR. AND MRS. WILLIAM SMITH
510 LIBERTY STREET
OAK PARK, ILLINOIS, 60011

Ordering Wedding Stationery

The invitation reflects the style of the wedding and lets guests know what to expect. An invitation should be factual and concise. It should say who, what, why, where, and when. Anything else is superfluous. In my opinion, the wedding invitation is not the place to be flowery—just give the facts and let expressions of love appear in the wedding vows. I feel the same way about hearts and flowers. These belong on the cake!

The best places to order stationery are a department store, a stationery store, or a jewelry store—preferably one that has an experienced consultant to advise you. Avoid ordering stationery in such places as drugstores, because they will print your order exactly as you give it to them—mistakes and all! I remember a couple who carefully checked the names for correct spelling and the date, but on the day of the wedding their phone rang off the hook because no one knew where the wedding was to take place. The couple had omitted this bit of information on their invitation!

There are many weights of paper, shades of color, sizes, and styles of script from which to choose. Think about the size of the invitation, especially if you intend to have something extra printed in the lower left corner, such as information about the reception or your new home address. The quantity of invitations depends on your guest count, plus an additional ten to twenty-five in case you discover people you have overlooked. It is much less expensive to get extras with your original order than to reorder! And remember: You'll need only one invitation per couple, not two.

Printing Processes

Hand engraving on copper plates is the most deluxe, expensive, and time-consuming printing process. Machine engraving (also done on copper plates) is difficult for anyone but an expert to differentiate from hand engraving. The most popular raised-lettering process, which is also much quicker and less expensive, is called thermography. Thermography gives the appearance of engraving: When you run your fingers over the paper, you can feel the raised letters. Offset printing is the least expensive process and is not usually used for wedding stationery.

Coat of Arms

If the family of the bride has a coat of arms and wishes to use it, the crest may be embossed at the top of the first page, but not in color. No other marking or device is acceptable. The crest is used only when the parents of the bride or her immediate family issue the invitation or announcement. The groom's full coat of arms is used only when the couple makes the announcement of their marriage.

When to Order and Mail

Invitations must be mailed four to six weeks before the wedding. Allow six weeks or more for mail to reach guests coming from a distance or from overseas.

Invitations, therefore, should be ordered at least two months before they will be sent. There may be a big rush of orders for the popular wedding months of June and September. Envelopes may be ordered in advance, however, so that they may be addressed, stamped, and ready for mailing before the actual invitations are received. Order extra envelopes; they will come in handy in case corrections are needed.

Proofreading

Ask the stationer to call you so that you can carefully proofread your order. Double-check names, addresses, sites, dates, times, and punctuation.

Stamps

For a personal touch, check with your post office for stamps suitable for use on wedding invitations and announcements. Stamps with birds, flowers, swans, or loving sentiments attract notice, and the recipients will be impressed with your attention to detail. Weigh a sample invitation with all enclosures to gauge the correct postage. This will help you avoid having all your invitations returned due to insufficient postage.

The Inner and Outer Envelope

Wedding invitations have two envelopes—an outer one and an inner one. The inner envelope is not sealed. The invitation, folded edge down, and all enclosures are put in the inner envelope, which bears only the names of invited guests, such as "Mr. and Mrs. Jackson," with no first names or addresses. Very intimate relatives may be addressed on the inner envelope in a loving way, such as "Grandmother" or "Aunt Joan and Uncle Paul." Small children's names are written simply "Curtis and Victoria" or, if the boy is under thirteen, "Miss Victoria and Master Curtis." (For unmarried females of any age, use "Miss.") A teenager's name should be written on a separate line below the parents' names: "Miss Victoria Jackson." The plural of "Miss" is "Misses," and the plural of "Mr." is "Messrs."—for example: "Misses Victoria and Alice Jackson" or "Messrs. Curtis and Richard Jackson." Even when young adults are living with their parents, it is courteous to send the young adults individual invitations. Other adult family members living under the same roof must also receive separate invitations.

The smaller inner envelope is inserted into the larger outer envelope so that the guest's name faces you when the outer envelope's flap is first opened. The inner envelope is always addressed by hand. Before addressing, avoid mixing up inner and outer envelopes! This could be a costly and time-consuming mistake.

How to Address Religious and Political Personages Socially

Official	Addressing Envelopes	Introduction	Place Card
Protestant clergy with degree	The Reverend Doctor Mark Potter and Mrs. Potter	Dr. Potter	Dr. Potter or Dr. Mark Potter
Protestant clergy without degree	The Reverend Mark Potter or The Reverend and Mrs. Mark Potter	Mr. Potter	Mr. Potter or Mr. Mark Potter
Bishop of the Episcopal Church	The Right Reverend Mark Potter and Mrs. Potter	Bishop Potter	Bishop Potter or Bishop Mark Potter
Bishop of the Methodist Church	The Reverend Mark Potter and Mrs. Potter	Bishop Potter	Bishop Potter or Bishop Mark Potter
Mormon Bishop	Mr. and Mrs. Mark Potter	Mr. Potter	Mr. Potter or Mr. Mark Potter
Roman Catholic Bishop or Archbishop	The Most Reverend Mark Potter	His Excellency	His Excellency Bishop Potter
Roman Catholic Monsignor	The Right Reverend Mark Potter	Monsignor Potter	Monsignor Potter or Monsignor Mark Potter
Roman Catholic Priest	The Reverend Father Mark Potter	Father Potter	Father Potter or Father Mark Potter
Roman Catholic Nun	Sister Mary Theresa or Diane Potter, R.S.C.J.	Sister Mary Theresa	Sister Mary Theresa or Sister Potter
Eastern Orthodox Communion Bishop or Priest	same as Roman Catholic	same as Roman Catholic	same as Roman Catholic
Rabbi	Rabbi David Solomon and Mrs. Solomon	Rabbi Solomon	Rabbi Solomon or Rabbi David Solomon
U.S. Senator	Senator and Mrs. Mark Potter	Senator or Senator Potter	Senator Potter or Senator Mark Potter
U.S. Representative	The Honorable Mark Potter and Mrs. Potter	Mr. Potter	The Honorable Mark Potter, Mr. Potter, or Mr. Mark Potter
Mayor	Mayor and Mrs. Mark Potter	Mayor Potter	The Mayor of Carmel
Judge	Judge and Mrs. Mark Potter	Judge Potter	Judge Potter or Judge Mark Potter

In addressing the outer envelope, no abbreviations or initials are used, except for the words "Mister" (use "Mr.") and "Mistress" (use "Mrs."). The words "street" and "avenue," as well as the name of the state, are also spelled out. See the example below:

> *Mr. and Mrs. Peter Jay Smith*
> *123 Lakeshore Road*
> *Saint James, Michigan 49720*

Return Address

There was a time when it was considered in poor taste to put return addresses on wedding invitations, but since the post office requests this information (and it also frowns on embossing), it is best to have the return address printed or legibly written on the top left corner of the envelope.

Wording of Invitations and Announcements

People who like to follow tradition may be surprised at the number of specific rules that are still in use today. Please, do not be misled by unusual examples found in some stationery sample albums.

1. The word "honour" (as in "honour of your presence") is still spelled with a *u* for a ceremony in a church or synagogue.

2. The wording for a ceremony in a home, club, or hotel is "request the pleasure of your company."

3. No punctuation is used except after abbreviations like "Mr.," "Mrs.," and "Jr." A comma is used after the day of the week: "Tuesday, the fifteenth of September." The title "Doctor" is written in full. Other abbreviations, initials, or nicknames are never used.

4. The year is optional on wedding invitations, but mandatory on announcements. If used, it must be spelled out. Long numbers in a street address, however, may be written in numerals. In a large city, there may be more than one church with the same name. To avoid confusion, give the church address on the invitation.

5. Half-hours are written as "half after four," never "half past four." The word "o'clock" is always spelled out.

6. An invitation to the wedding ceremony in church does not include an R.S.V.P., unless followed by a reception, but an invitation to a home wedding always includes an R.S.V.P. ("R.S.V.P." stands for the French phrase *répondez s'il vous plaît,* which means "Please respond.")

7. On the reception invitation, "R.S.V.P." or "The favour of a reply is requested" are both correct. If the address to which the reply is to be sent differs from the address on the invitation, you may print, "Kindly send reply to . . ." and include the zip code with the address. Always give a *street address* to which guests should respond; never give a telephone number or e-mail address.

I am also frequently asked if the name of a deceased parent of the bride or groom may be put on the wedding invitation. Although a deceased parent is frequently mentioned in a newspaper announcement, he or she is never mentioned on a wedding invitation or announcement.

Choice of Menu

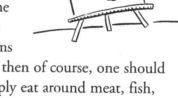

There are two schools of thought regarding choice of menu pertaining to a wedding invitation. One school believes that the host should plan the meal, as one would in one's own home, without asking guests what they would like to eat. When a guest informs the host of a restricted diet for reasons of health, then of course, one should oblige. Most people feel that vegetarians can simply eat around meat, fish, or fowl and that no mention of menu need be made on the invitation.

The second school of thought follows the recommendation of caterers, who suggest offering a choice of food, as is done when there are meetings, conventions, and so on, or when people are paying for their own meal. Unfortunately, this example has crept into purely social functions as well. If you decide to offer a choice for vegetarians, then put that information on the response card, or serve a buffet meal instead of a full-service sit-down dinner.

Who Is Hosting the Wedding

Traditionally, the parents of the bride hosted the wedding, invitations were sent out in their name, and guests knew whom to thank. Today, a wedding's financial arrangements may not be so clear. When the bride's or groom's parents are divorced, several family members, such as a grandmother, aunt, and/or the bride and groom, may all chip in and offer to share some of the expenses. This poses a problem when deciding who will issue the invitation.

It is best to limit the hosts on the invitation to not more than one or two couples, such as the bride and groom's parents, or two divorced parents. One needs to be magnanimous in making these delicate decisions. There are other ways one may honor a person, such as with a corsage, by inviting him or her to be in a wedding photograph, and so on. The suggestions on the following pages provide guidance for wording on invitations to address various family situations.

Parents of the Bride

> *Mr. and Mrs. Loren Jay Lovejoy*
> *request the honour of your presence*
> *at the marriage of their daughter*
> *Jennifer Anne*
> *to*
> *Mr. Robert William Baldwin*
> *on Saturday, the sixteenth of September*
> *two thousand*
> *at five o'clock*
> *Congregational Church*
> *Berkeley, California*

Including the year is optional on the wedding invitation, but it is obligatory on the announcement. The year must be spelled out.

Parents of the Bride and Groom

> *Mr. and Mrs. Loren Jay Lovejoy*
> *request the pleasure of your company*
> *at the marriage of their daughter*
> *Jennifer Anne*
> *to*
> *Robert William Baldwin*
> *son of*
> *Mr. and Mrs. Roger James Baldwin*

Note that no "Mr." is used before the groom's name when his parents are also being mentioned on the invitation.

If the Bride's Mother Is Widowed

> Mrs. Loren Jay Lovejoy
> requests the honour of your presence
> at the marriage of her daughter

If the Bride's Mother Is Divorced

> Mrs. Diane Jones Lovejoy
> requests the honour of your presence
> at the marriage of her daughter

If the Bride's Mother Is Remarried

> Mr. and Mrs. Alexander Glen Wilson
> request the honour of your presence
> at the marriage of her daughter
> Jennifer Anne Lovejoy

If the Bride's Divorced Parents Are Both Remarried and Are Cohosting the Wedding

If the bride's mother and father are divorced and both have remarried, and the parents are friendly and wish to share the wedding expenses and act as cohosts, then both names appear on the invitation. The bride's mother's name appears first:

> Mr. and Mrs. Alexander Glen Wilson
> and
> Mr. and Mrs. Loren Jay Lovejoy
> request the honour of your presence
> at the marriage of
> Jennifer Anne Lovejoy

However, it is more common that only the bride's mother issues the invitations to the wedding. The father might issue the invitations to the reception if he is paying for it. In this case, the two invitations would be mailed together in one envelope.

A problem with sending an invitation by both sets of parents—even if they are cohosting the wedding—is how to refer to their daughter. Wedding invitations should not raise questions; they should always be clear to the recipients. Therefore, the following wording is not recommended:

> *Mr. and Mrs. Loren Jay Lovejoy*
> *and*
> *Mr. and Mrs. Alexander Glen Wilson*
> *request the honour of your presence*
> *at the marriage of their daughter*

Whose daughter, exactly, is getting married?

If the Bride's Father Is a Widower

> *Mr. Loren Jay Lovejoy*
> *requests the honour of your presence*
> *at the marriage of his daughter*

If the Bride's Father Is a Remarried Widower

> *Mr. and Mrs. Loren Jay Lovejoy*
> *request the honour of your presence*
> *at the marriage of his daughter*

If a Young Bride Is Marrying for the Second Time

If a young bride is marrying for the second time and her parents are sending the invitation, her married name is included. However, do not include the word "Mrs." in front of her name. See the following example:

> *Mr. and Mrs. Loren Jay Lovejoy*
> *request the honour of your presence*
> *at the marriage of their daughter*
> *Jennifer Lovejoy Baldwin*

Q&A

Dear Edith,
We are having problems in the wording of our wedding invitations. My mother and stepfather are hosting the wedding, but my father is going to walk me down the aisle.

ANSWER: You may use your mother and stepfather's names on the invitation and list your father's name on the wedding program as a member of the wedding party:

Mr. and Mrs. Loren Jay Lovejoy
request the honour of your presence
at the marriage of her daughter

As host, your stepfather has the choice of standing in the receiving line or circulating among the guests.

Sometimes divorced parents who are sharing wedding expenses may be perfectly willing to send invitations from both the mother and the father of the bride. In this case, the mother's name comes first and the word "and" is omitted.

Mrs. Loren Jay Lovejoy
Mr. Alexander Glen Wilson
request the honour of your presence
at the marriage of their daughter

Your decision should satisfy your feelings as well as the feelings of your parents and stepfather.

The wedding invitation may also be issued by a friend, elder sibling, grandparent, aunt, uncle, or any other close relative. For a second marriage, the bride may choose to limit attendance at the ceremony to family and special friends. It is especially thoughtful to include any young children of the bride or groom in the wedding party. (See Chapter Eight.) There is no limit to the number of people who may be invited to the reception.

Military Titles

When the bride, groom, or any parent is a member of the U.S. Army, Navy, Coast Guard, Air Force, or Marine Corps or is on active duty in any of the military reserves, his or her military title is used. Place the title in front of the name for an army officer whose rank is captain or higher or for a naval officer whose rank is lieutenant, senior grade, or higher. For example:

> *Colonel Richard Cromwell*
> *United States Army*

For those of lower rank, state name and title as follows. (Note that first and second lieutenants in the U.S. Army both use only the word "lieutenant.")

> *Richard Cromwell*
> *Ensign, United States Navy*

For reserve officers on active duty, the second line should read:

> *Army of the United States*
> *or*
> *United States Naval Reserve*

For a noncommissioned officer or enlisted person, you may state rank and branch of the service below his or her name if desired. For example:

> *Richard Cromwell*
> *Corporal, Signal Corps, United States Army*
> *or*
> *Richard Cromwell*
> *Apprentice Seaman, United States Naval Reserve*

High-ranking officers of the regular armed forces continue to use their titles, followed by their branch of service, even after retirement.

A bride who is in the service may use her military title if she wishes. When her parents issue the invitation, she should be referred to as follows:

> *Nancy Olive*
> *Lieutenant, United States Army*

When the bride and groom issue their own invitation, it should read:

> *Nancy Olive MacArthur*
> *Lieutenant, United States Army*

Other Titles

Medical doctors, dentists, veterinarians, and all persons ordinarily called by their titles should use them on wedding invitations. One holding an academic degree does not use a title unless he or she holds an extremely high position and is always referred to that way. If someone is due to receive a medical degree by the time the wedding takes place, the title should be used on the invitation.

Traditionally, neither the bride nor the bride's mother would use the title "Doctor" on a wedding invitation; however, this is changing. If both the bride and groom are medical doctors, the invitation will read:

> *Dr. Jennifer Anne Lovejoy*
> *and*
> *Dr. Charles Alexander Wilson*

If the bride is a medical doctor and the groom is not:

> *Dr. Jennifer Anne Lovejoy*
> *and*
> *Mr. Charles Alexander Wilson*

If the groom's parents are also listed on the invitation, omit titles from the names of the bride and groom:

> *Jennifer Anne Lovejoy*
> *and*
> *Charles Alexander Wilson*
> *son of*
> *Mr. and Mrs. George Charles Wilson*

If the bride's father has a title, use it on the invitation:

> *Justice and Mrs. Loren Jay Lovejoy*

When the bride's mother uses a professional title both professionally and socially, the couple is correctly referred to as:

> *Senator Barbara Lovejoy and Mr. Loren Jay Lovejoy*

If you feel that the above sample looks awkward all on one line, you may separate the names:

> *Senator Barbara Lovejoy*
> *and*
> *Mr. Loren Jay Lovejoy*
> *request the honour of your presence*

You may also simply use:

> *Mr. and Mrs. Loren Jay Lovejoy*

When the Groom's Family Hosts the Wedding

When the groom's parents issue the invitations, use this wording:

> *Mr. and Mrs. Loren Jay Lovejoy*
> *request the honour of your presence*
> *at the marriage of*
> *Miss Gloria Niswander*
> *to their son*
> *Henry Loren Lovejoy*

When it comes to announcements, however, these should be sent in the name of the bride's parents, if they are living. If they wish, the groom's parents may send their friends personal notes with newspaper clippings instead of announcements.

Invitations by Both the Bride's and Groom's Parents

When the bride's and groom's parents cohost the wedding and share in the expenses, it is only fair that both couples' names appear on the invitations:

> *Mr. and Mrs. Loren Jay Lovejoy*
> *and*
> *Mr. and Mrs. Alexander Glen Wilson*
> *request the pleasure of your company*
> *at the marriage of*
> *Jennifer Anne Lovejoy*
> *and*
> *Charles Alexander Wilson*

Foreign Countries

Invitation customs differ in Europe and other foreign countries, and their delightful practice is sometimes followed here. For example, an invitation may be printed in English on the right side and in Spanish or another language on the left side of a folded invitation. Or both the bride and groom's parents may issue a double invitation as follows:

Mr. and Mrs. Napoleon Quintanilla	*Mr. and Mrs. Christopher Smith*
request the honour of your	*request the honour of your*
presence at the marriage of	*presence at the marriage of*
their daughter	*their son*
Carolina	*Walter*
to	*to*
Mr. Walter Arnold Smith	*Miss Carolina Quintanilla*

Double Weddings

When two sisters have a double ceremony, the older sister is mentioned first and the invitation reads:

> *Mr. and Mrs. Loren Jay Lovejoy*
> *request the honour of your presence*
> *at the marriage of their daughters*
> *Jennifer Anne*
> *to*
> *Mr. Robert William Baldwin*
> *and*
> *Glenna Julia*
> *to*
> *Mr. Gregory Charles Fitzpatrick*

If the brides are not sisters, the parents' names are listed in alphabetical order.

Your Own Invitations

There are numerous occasions when couples prefer to issue their own invitations. When both the bride and groom are living away from their hometowns and have set up lives of their own, the word "Miss" is used before the bride's name. The invitation should read as follows:

> *The honour of your presence*
> *is requested*
> *at the marriage of*
> *Miss Jennifer Ann Lovejoy*
> *to (or and)*
> *Mr. Jackson Ray Dilworth*

For a second marriage not in a church, the invitation should read:

> *The pleasure of your company*
> *is requested*
> *at the marriage of*
> *Jennifer Lovejoy Baldwin*
> *to (or and)*
> *Jackson Ray Dilworth*

If the bride and groom choose to send invitations in their own name, yet wish to include parents, stepparents, and/or estranged parents, they may use the following form:

> *Miss Jennifer Ann Lovejoy*
> *and*
> *Mr. Jackson Ray Dilworth*
> *together with their families*
> *request the honour of your presence*

Out-of-Town Receptions by Parents

When one set of parents lives in a community other than that in which the wedding will take place, and those parents wish to have their friends meet the bride and groom, they may plan a reception for the newlyweds either before or after the wedding. The wording on the invitation may be either formal or informal.

The example below uses formal wording for a reception to be held before the wedding:

> *Mr. and Mrs. Loren Jay Lovejoy*
> *request the pleasure of your company*
> *at a buffet supper in honor of*
> *Miss Jennifer Anne Lovejoy*
> *and*
> *Mr. Robert William Baldwin*
> *on Saturday, the fifteenth of October*
> *at seven o'clock*
> *Rolling Hills Country Club*
> *Kansas City*
>
> *The favour of a reply is requested.*   *Black Tie*

The following example of informal wording might be used on a foldover invitation to a reception to be held after the wedding:

(outside)

> *Mr. and Mrs. Loren Jay Lovejoy*

(inside)

> *You are cordially invited*
> *to a cocktail reception*
> *in honour of*
> *Jennifer and Robert Baldwin*
> *on Wednesday, the fifth of June*
> *from five until seven o'clock*
> *100 Greenway Drive*
>
> *Regrets only*
> or
> *Please reply*

Additional Information

In Case of Rain

If an alternate site has been planned in case of rain for an outdoor wedding or reception, this information may be shown on the bottom right corner of the invitation.

For a Catholic Wedding

If the wedding will be a nuptial mass, it is considerate to state this on the bottom right corner of the invitation to give guests an idea of how long the service will be.

Insert Cards

There are numerous cards that may be inserted into the fold of an invitation: reception invitations, pew cards, response cards, and at-home cards. When one uses insert cards, it is best to use folded invitations, because when invitations are not folded, insert cards are sometimes left unnoticed inside the envelopes. This may result in hurt feelings when people think they have not been invited to the reception.

Reception Invitation

When the reception takes place immediately after the ceremony at the same location, you may print on the bottom left corner of the invitation: "Reception immediately following ceremony."

When the reception is held at a different location from the ceremony, a separate card is inserted with the invitation. If it is to be a breakfast, brunch, luncheon, cocktail supper, buffet, or dinner, it is considerate to say so explicitly. Grateful guests will be able to plan their schedules accordingly. A sample reception card may read as follows:

> *Judge and Mrs. Edwin Eisendrath II*
> *request the pleasure of your company*
> *at a wedding breakfast*
> *following the ceremony*
> *Pierre Hotel*
> *New York City*
>
> *R.S.V.P.*

Or the card may read:

> *Reception and Dinner*
> *immediately following the ceremony*
> *Berkshire Country Club*
> *Rolling Hills, Kentucky*
>
> *The favour of a reply is requested*
> *Old Orchard Lane*
> *Blue Lake, Kentucky*

When one provides a response card, it is not necessary to print "R.S.V.P" or "The favour of a reply is requested" on the reception invitation. The response card is obviously a request for an answer.

The Response Card

This little 3½-by-5-inch card has crept into our lifestyles for the convenience of both guests and hosts. It prompts guests to reply sooner, and it gives the host an exact head count. An exact count is imperative for two reasons: (1) The caterer charges the host for the contracted number of guests, whether or not those guests attend (and this charge can add up mightily if guests are lackadaisical with their responses); and (2) When there is a sit-down dinner with place cards, it is very unpleasant for a guest to be seated next to a vacant chair. The response card comes with a matching envelope, which should have a return address printed on it. The envelope may or may not be stamped. The response card may read as follows:

> *The favour of a reply is requested*
> *by June 1, 2000* (date optional)
>
> M _____
>
>   *will* _____ *attend*

Or it may read:

> *Please respond on or before July 1, 2000* (date optional)
>
> M _____
>
>   *will* _____ *attend*

The card may also simply read "Please respond" at the top. This leaves room for a guest to write a personal note.

What about the Kids?

Based on the astounding number of internet questions I have received regarding the matter of kids at weddings, I can truthfully say that people seem to be more concerned with the issue of children at weddings than almost any other issue. Although some weddings lend themselves nicely to having the whole family in attendance, and some couples even thoughtfully provide a baby-sitting service, it is understandable why many couples prefer to invite adult guests only.

Since each guest receives an explicit invitation to a wedding, it should be clear to guests that they may not bring youngsters along unless the children's names are mentioned on the invitations. Unfortunately, this rule is sometimes ignored, and you can't count on your wishes being passed along by word of mouth.

Consequently, invitations to an adults-only reception must state clearly, "Reception and Dinner for Adult Guests" or "Dinner for Adult Guests

Following the Ceremony" on the lower left corner of the reception card. This is especially important when one is planning a formal seated dinner.

In case of doubt, guests may check with the host, who might say, "I am sorry, but space does not permit us to include children, except those in the wedding party." Expect some flack, but once your decision is made, it is best to stand firm.

Another option for indicating that children are not included is to print the following on the response card:

> *Number of Adults*_____
>   *M*_____
> *will*_____*attend.*

On the other hand, if you wish to include children, you might request the following information on the response card:

> *Babysitter provided*
> *Number of children's meals*_____

The Address on the Response Envelope

The address on the response envelope indicates where the acceptance is to be sent—and where wedding presents are sent as well. If the bride lives in one city and her parents live in another city, it is best to have the response go to the city where the wedding is to take place, since some people will be slow to respond.

Pew Cards

For very large weddings, this little 2-by-3-inch card invites special guests or close relatives to be seated in a reserved pew marked with ribbons or flowers. (Seats are not numbered or otherwise assigned within these rows.) On the card is printed "Within the ribbon" or "Groom's reserved section." Instead of a printed pew card, the host of the wedding may sign his or her name on a calling card with all the necessary information written on the back. The pew card is mailed after guests have accepted the invitation to the wedding. A printed pew card may also read:

```
will present this card to the usher
Blessed Sacrament Cathedral
Pew Number
```

At-Home Cards

These are usually ordered at the same time as the invitations and
announcements, and they may be included with the invitations or the
announcements. At-home cards give the newlyweds' new street address,
city, state, and zip code. It is not necessary to send at-home cards unless
the couple is permanently settled. When the at-home card is included in
the wedding invitation, it reads as follows:

```
After the first of August
Old Orchard Lane
Houston, Texas 77000
```

When the at-home card is included with the announcement, it
includes the couple's name:

```
Mr. and Mrs. Robert William Baldwin
after the first of August
Old Orchard Lane
Houston, Texas 77000
```

Instead of sending a separate card, one may put the date and address
on the lower left corner of the announcement.

Wedding Announcements

These are mailed only to people who have not been invited to the wedding, yet whom you would like to inform of the marriage. In the case of a
home wedding, for example, the number of guests may have to be limited
to a small group. Announcements may be mailed to people who live far
away or acquaintances you have not seen in a long time. A wedding
announcement does not require a gift, so there is no need to hesitate in
sending one. Wedding announcements, addressed in the same manner as

invitations, may be sent by the parents of the bride, by parents of both the bride and groom, by any close relative, or by the couple themselves. An announcement sent by the parents of the bride for a church or synagogue wedding might read:

> *Mr. and Mrs. Loren Jay Lovejoy*
> *have the honour of*
> *announcing the marriage of their daughter*
> *Jennifer Anne Lovejoy*
> *and*
> *Mr. Robert William Baldwin*
> *on Saturday, the seventh of October*
> *two thousand*
> *at five o'clock*
> *Saint Margaret's Church*
> *Saint Louis, Missouri*

Please note that the fifth line says "and" rather than "to." Remember that an announcement must state the year. The time and location, however, are optional.

Announcements sent by both sets of parents for a wedding in church or synagogue might read:

> *Mr. and Mrs. Loren Jay Lovejoy*
> *and*
> *Mr. and Mrs. Richard Albert Baldwin*
> *have the honour of*
> *announcing the marriage of*
> *Jennifer Anne Lovejoy*
> *and*
> *Robert William Baldwin*
> *on Saturday, the seventh of October*
> *at five o'clock*
> *two thousand*
> *Saint Margaret's Church*
> *Saint Louis, Missouri*

Please note that "Mr." is not used in the announcement above, because the groom's parents as well as the bride's are announcing the marriage.

Dear Edith,

We are inviting two hundred relatives and friends to our Florida wedding and are now ordering our invitations.

I live in Chicago and would like to notify some of my friends at work and members of my basketball team that I am married. However, I don't want to send them invitations, because I know that they can't come to the wedding and they would feel obligated to send a gift.

Should I write a note, telephone them when I get back, or skip the whole thing?

ANSWER: Order announcements when you order invitations. Announcements are mailed immediately after the wedding, do not require a gift, and meet your needs perfectly.

Announcements sent by parents of the bride to a wedding service not held in a place of worship should use the word "pleasure" instead of "honour":

Mr. and Mrs. Loren Jay Lovejoy
have the pleasure of
announcing the marriage of their daughter
Jennifer Anne Lovejoy
and
Mr. Robert William Baldwin
on Saturday, the seventh of October
two thousand
Saint Louis, Missouri

Announcements issued by a couple themselves will read as follows:

> *Miss Jennifer Anne Lovejoy*
> *and*
> *Mr. Robert William Baldwin*
> *announce their marriage*
> *on Sunday, the fourteenth of February*
> *two thousand*
> *Palm Beach, Florida*

A Death in the Immediate Family

When a very old person, such as a grandparent, has requested that a wedding go on as planned in the event of his or her death, then the wedding may take place as originally scheduled.

If there is a sudden tragic death in the immediate family and the wedding must be postponed, a notice may be sent at once to the newspaper, and the invitations may be recalled by telephone or telegram. If time permits, a printed card may be sent. Including the names of the bride and groom on such a card is optional.

> *Mr. and Mrs. James Longworth Phillips*
> *regret that due to a death in the family*
> *the invitation to*
> *their daughter's wedding*
> *on Saturday, the fourth of June*
> *must be recalled*

Invitations to a large wedding may be recalled, and the wedding may still take place with only a few close friends and relatives present. Much depends on the feelings of the immediate family.

Multipurpose Informals

These small foldover notes with envelopes are used for a great many purposes. They may be used as thank-you notes for shower and wedding gifts and also as invitations to small, informal weddings. If the notes will be used before the wedding, the bride's name or premarriage initials may be engraved or imprinted on the cover. For notes used after the wedding, the bride's new name or initials are used. A popular new custom is to print the couple's surname initial large and centered, with smaller initials for the bride's and groom's given names on either side.

Wedding Program

The popularity of printed wedding programs is on the rise, and for good reason. Since more and more families and friends gather from afar, and fewer and fewer weddings bring people together who all know each other, it is helpful to list the names of the wedding party in a program. It is also nice to be able to refer to the names of the soloist, organist, and officiant.

There is no prescribed form for wedding programs. The cover may show a picture of the church or temple with such words as:

> *The Service of Marriage*
> *of*
> *Jennifer Anne Lovejoy*
> *and*
> *Robert William Baldwin*
> *on*
> *Saturday, the third of June*
> *two thousand*
> *at six o'clock in the evening*

The order of service, including musical selections, may be printed on the inside cover. On the opposite page may be a list of names of members of the wedding party. If a beloved relative has passed away, it is appropriate to mention him or her here.

The back page may be blank or may have a map guiding guests to the reception site, or it may feature a message or quotation from a favorite poem of the bride and groom that pays tribute to a deceased relative.

If one wishes, one may request in the program that no flash pictures be taken during the ceremony.

It is advisable not to have the program printed too far in advance, as there are usually some last-minute changes, particularly in musical selections. Do check with your clergyperson, as he or she may be helpful in having the program printed.

Q&A

Dear Edith,

I would like to design a program listing the names of the members of the wedding party, their relationships to the bride and groom, the name of the clergyperson, the soloist, and the musical selections. We are having a home wedding and sit-down dinner in the garden. Do you have any suggestions?

ANSWER: *You might consider using a 4¼-by-5½-inch foldover card with an attractive and appropriate floral or scenic design on the cover. Each guest's name can be written in calligraphy on the cover, thereby using the foldover also as a place card. You can staple an insert inside the foldover, which gives you extra pages.*

Here you may give the time, date, and place of the wedding. On a separate page, there will be enough room to include the dinner menu, in addition to the names of the wedding party, clergyperson, soloist, and musical program. You may also include a personalized message, poem, or quote in the foldover.

To dress up the foldover, you can take a narrow ribbon and tie it with a bow or fancy knot along the crease.

Your local print shop may be able to help you choose the quality of paper, lettering, and colors. Insist that you proof the copy before it is printed, and proof it carefully before giving your approval.

Wedding Weekend Guide

When a number of guests come from afar and there are several events planned for the wedding weekend, it is helpful to compile this information, along with things to see and do, for each visitor. This may be done on the computer, giving the time, place, and directions for each event, as well as a name and phone number of someone in charge of arrangements.

A response card with a blank for accepting or regretting a cocktail party, rehearsal dinner, museum tour, softball or golf game, pool party, picnic, or afterglow may be mailed ahead to each guest or enclosed with the wedding invitation.

Printed Souvenir Menus

At formal luncheons or dinners, a menu of the meal may be placed on each table. This may be hand-lettered or printed and artistically decorated with a floral pattern if desired. Individual souvenir menus may also be placed on the plate in front of each guest. I have even seen an interesting souvenir menu printed in green on a 4-by-11-inch yellow ribbon of silk, with the name of the hotel and crest, the bride and groom's name, the menu, the wines, and, at the very bottom, the city and date.

Printed Acknowledgment Cards

For very large weddings, it is helpful to have cards printed to acknowledge the receipt of gifts. The bride and groom, then, are not under such heavy pressure to immediately write their personal thank-you cards. The card may say:

> *Mr. and Mrs. Baldwin*
> *have received your wedding gift and*
> *will take pleasure in writing you*
> *later of their appreciation.*

Thank-You Notes

Here are some helpful tips to remember when writing a thank-you note:

1. Write the date on the note. Sometimes mail is delayed through no fault of yours.

2. Mention the the gift specifically. The giver would like to know that you remember this particular gift and whom it came from.

3. Mention something nice about the gift. If the only thing you like about the gift is the design or color, then mention the design or color.

4. Mention your fiancé(e)'s name.

5. Sign only one name to the note, since only one person actually writes it. Be warm and friendly in closing by writing "Love," "Affectionately," or "Cordially." "Sincerely" sounds too cold.

6. Mail thank-you notes as soon as possible, or givers may become anxious that their gifts have gone astray.

May 15, 2000

Dear Connie,

Richard and I are thrilled with the brass candleholder! The Early American design will be absolutely perfect in our new home. Thank you so much for this lovely gift.

Affectionately,
Jennifer

Oct. 1, 2000

Dear Jim,

Betty and I are enjoying the coffee grinder you gave us so much! We both thank you for your useful gift and hope you will be able to share a good cup of coffee with us soon. Our best wishes to you and Jane.

Cordially,
Bill

Determining Names after Marriage

This is a good time to devote some thought to the names the bride and groom will use after marriage.

Taking the Groom's Surname

In the past, it has been the social custom that when Jennifer Anne Lovejoy married Robert William Baldwin, she took her husband's surname and began signing herself as either Mrs. Robert Baldwin or Jennifer Lovejoy Baldwin. Many couples agree that this is still the best choice today.

Other Options

However, there are also many couples who do not agree with this custom, and they do have other options. It is not generally known that a married woman is entitled—but not legally compelled—to use her husband's surname. No state in the United States (except Hawaii) has a law stating that a woman must take her husband's name upon marriage. Even less well known is the fact that a married man is not legally compelled to retain his original surname.

Several additional options for postmarriage names are described below. Discuss all the options—traditional and modern—with your future spouse and choose whichever is best for you. You may even come up with an option not described here. Do not worry about the opinions of others regarding your names. You and your spouse should choose names that are meaningful and comfortable for *you.*

Do remember that a name change may require a change in many personal documents. Look into requirements for driver's licenses, car registrations, bank accounts, vault box access, Social Security cards, credit cards, insurance policies, leases, deeds, property titles, passports, voter registrations, wills, stock certificates, post office listings, school/alumni listings, utility accounts, tax identification, and any other official business you may be involved in. To save time in notification, you can have cards printed with new name information for enclosure with correspondence, bills, and so on.

Keeping Your Own Name

A professional man or woman may feel that it is important to keep the name with which he or she has become identified. By assuming a new name, he or she may suffer a loss of identity and create confusion among customers, clients, or constituents. Some people may simply desire to keep their own names to acknowledge the heritage their names convey. A man or woman's birth-given name may be retained legally on any official documents and passed on to children.

If the bride and groom both choose to retain their birth-given names, it may be helpful to enclose a card with the invitations and/or announcements. (Many people may simply assume that newlyweds will take the groom's surname.) The card may also include the at-home address and may read as follows:

> *Jennifer Anne Lovejoy*
> *and*
> *Robert William Baldwin*
> *wish to announce that they*
> *will retain their birth-given names*
> *for all legal and social purposes*
> *after their marriage*
> *The understanding and cooperation*
> *of friends and relatives would*
> *be greatly appreciated*
>
> *After the first of July*
> *323 Bridge Street*
> *Portland, Maine 04110*

Changing Your Middle Name

Some people may choose to change their middle names after marriage. This allows one to retain a birth-given name while acknowledging connection to a new spouse. One may keep a birth-given surname and assume the spouse's surname as a middle name. Another option is to use one's birth-given surname as a middle name and assume the spouse's surname. Jennifer Anne Lovejoy, therefore, might become Jennifer Baldwin Lovejoy or Jennifer Lovejoy Baldwin.

Hyphenated Names

Some couples adopt hyphenated names. For example, Jennifer Anne Lovejoy and Robert William Baldwin may become Jennifer Anne Lovejoy-Baldwin and Robert William Lovejoy-Baldwin. The surnames may be placed in either order. Be aware that some computers may not be programmed to accept hyphenated names, in which case it is necessary to insist that records be hand-typed.

Taking the Bride's Surname

Many people are not aware that this is an option, but it is! Although the practice is still uncommon, some couples do choose it.

Save-the-Date Letters

When invited guests are coming from afar, it is thoughtful to send them a save-the-date letter long in advance of the wedding invitation, giving information about the community where the wedding will take place. Often, family and friends plan vacations around the wedding date, and it is necessary to make reservations early. A sample form letter might read as follows:

Dear Family and Friends,

We are delighted to let you know that our daughter Jennifer will marry Robert Baldwin on July 16, 2000. You will be receiving a formal invitation in June.

Since the wedding will take place in a popular summer resort, we wish to provide you with helpful information regarding travel and lodgings. Enclosed you will find the names, addresses, telephone numbers, and rates of selected hotels and motels, as well as airline schedules, maps, and recreation information.

If you have any questions or need further details, please call or write us.

Fondly,
Loren Jay Lovejoy

P.S. Please let us know if you would like us to arrange for your lodgings with some of our friends.

Checklist of Choices for Stationery Trousseau
Wedding Invitations

- For fewer than twenty-five guests: handwritten on foldover informal notes or on cards enclosed in envelopes
- For more than twenty-five guests: thermography, engraving, or calligraphy reproduction with inner and outer envelopes

- Acknowledgment cards (for very large weddings only)
- Possible matching inserts:
  - response cards and envelopes
  - reception cards
  - pew cards
  - at-home cards

Wedding Announcements

- For fewer than twenty-five guests: handwritten notes with the option of enclosing a reprint of a newspaper clipping
- For more than twenty-five guests: thermography, engraving, or calligraphy reproduction with envelopes

Wedding Program

- Usually printed, but not too far in advance

Multipurpose Informals or Thank-You Notes

- Foldover notes or cards with envelopes, with monogram or name on cover (thermography, engraving, or calligraphy)

Place Cards

- Handwritten or lettered with calligraphy

Souvenir Menus

- Handwritten, calligraphy reproductions, or printed. Borders may have original artwork or coloring. Menus may be rolled and tied with colorful ribbons and flowers.

Wedding Party Guide

- Folders giving the time, place and directions to prenuptial events— rehearsal, rehearsal dinner, wedding, reception, and so on.

Notes

Chapter Eight

Attendants in the Wedding Party

Laughter is the sunshine of our soul.

RALPH WALDO EMERSON

Choosing Your Attendants

Choosing the attendants for a wedding can at times be very simple, pleasant, and uncomplicated. It is so easy for the bride to invite a best friend or sister to be maid or matron of honor, or for the groom to invite a brother or best friend to be his best man. In the South, the father is often invited to be the groom's best man.

There are times, however, when complications arise that require creative solutions. Let's suppose the bride has twin sisters. Or the groom is one of triplets. Or the bride's best friend announces she is pregnant, and her due date coincides with the wedding date. Or one of the attendants is transferred out of the country. When marrying for the second time, a father may want both his sons to share equally in the ceremony.

What to do?

It is perfectly possible to have two maids or matrons of honor or two best men. They share all responsibilities, the older having first choice. When the bride or groom has a young brother or sister between the ages of five and ten, he or she may be included as flower girl or ring bearer at a formal wedding. Young nieces, nephews, or children from a previous marriage will also feel very special to be included as part of the wedding party. Boys and girls over ten may be invited to be junior bridesmaids or groomsmen.

A bride or groom need not feel compelled to ask a friend to be an attendant just because the friend had the bride or groom as an attendant in his or her wedding. Friends should understand that it may be a small wedding or that the bride and groom may wish to include more relatives in the wedding party.

It sometimes poses a financial difficulty for attendants to pay for their own outfits. The bride and groom may bring up the matter and offer, if they wish, to pay for half or all of the outfit, and the subject need not be discussed with other members of the wedding party.

New Trends

Some brides choose to ask a close male friend to be their honored attendant, and by the same token, some grooms choose to ask a woman to be their honored attendant. When a person of the opposite sex is chosen as an honored attendant, he or she wears the same attire as the other attendants of his or her sex. The bridesman accompanies the bridesmaids down the aisle and stands with them during the ceremony, and the grooms-woman stands with the groomsmen. There are no firm guidelines when it comes to walking down or back up the aisle. They may walk alone, or two or three attendants may walk together.

The duties of the bridesman and the groomswoman are similar to the traditional duties of the maid or matron of honor and best man: that is, to give encouragement and support to the bride and groom as described below. There may be some limits when it comes to attending all-female showers or all-male bachelor parties. It would also, of course, be awkward for the bridesman to assist the bride in getting dressed, as well as for the grooms-woman to assist the groom in getting dressed. A bridesmaid or groomsman could assume this task instead.

A Word of Caution

In the excitement of being newly engaged, some couples hastily choose their attendants, and here I must offer a word of caution. Do not choose your attendants a year ahead! Circumstances change. People move, are transferred out of the country, and get married, pregnant, or divorced. (A divorced woman, by the way, would be a maid—not a matron—of honor.) A person you are close to today may not be the one you would choose six months from now or vice versa. Six months ahead is time enough to ask a relative or friend to be an attendant. If someone pressures you for an answer before you are ready, just say you have not crossed that bridge yet.

When someone drops out of the wedding party due to unforeseen circumstances, it is perfectly acceptable to have an uneven number of male and female attendants.

The Duties of the Maid or Matron of Honor

The most important duty of the maid or matron of honor is to be supportive to the bride before and on the wedding day. She may be invited to shop with the bride or assist in addressing invitations and announcements. She is invited to all the parties and may give one herself. She is obliged to purchase a bridesmaid's dress and shoes selected by the bride. She will also choose a wedding gift for the couple and attend the rehearsal.

On the wedding day, the maid or matron of honor arrives early at the bride's house and helps the bride dress, gives her encouragement, and soothes frayed nerves. She will keep track of the hour and do what she can to get everyone to the ceremony on time. When a wedding takes place at home or in the garden, she remembers to take the telephone off the hook during the ceremony. If there is a double-ring ceremony, she holds the groom's ring and hands it to the bride. She also signs her name to the marriage license as a witness. During a more formal wedding, she holds the bride's bouquet, helps adjust her veil, and rearranges the bride's train when she turns to leave at the end of the service. She stands next to the couple in the receiving line. At the reception, she is seated on the groom's left at the head table.

After the reception, the maid or matron of honor escorts the bride to her dressing room and helps her pack and change into her going-away outfit. Then she brings the bride's parents in to say their private good-byes and thank-yous before the couple leave for their honeymoon. She may suggest

Dear Edith,
I have been asked to be a maid of honor. I have a full-time job, and the bride lives in another city. What are my responsibilities?

ANSWER: The bride knew the circumstances when she asked you to be her maid of honor. In addition to writing frequent words of cheer, investing in a bridesmaid dress and shoes, selecting a wedding gift, and attending the rehearsal, your primary responsibility is to be supportive before and on the day of the wedding.

the bride prepare a greeting card to give her parents, grandparents, or a special relative, along with a hug, before leaving the reception.

The Duties of the Best Man

Next to the bride and groom, the best man is the most important member of the wedding party on the day of the wedding. It is he who lightens the groom's load. The best man is responsible for the groom being dressed and on time for the ceremony. He is in charge of keeping the bride's wedding ring until the officiant asks for it. He keeps the wedding license and the officiant's fee in his own pocket. If the officiant is a minister, the best man sees that the check is made out to the minister—not the church—and delivers the check in an envelope before the ceremony or immediately afterward. He may also distribute envelopes containing payments to the organist, soloist, sexton, and/or acolytes. He signs the marriage license as a witness. The couple is not legally married until the officiant, the bride and groom, and two witnesses sign the marriage license.

Just before a church ceremony, the best man enters from the vestry immediately after the groom and stands next to him so that he can conveniently give the wedding ring to the groom when the minister calls for it. At the end of the service, he may either walk out with the maid or matron of honor or leave through a side door while the procession goes up the aisle. He goes quickly to the front of the church, gives the groom his hat and coat, if needed, and helps the bride and groom into their car. Unless there is a driver, the best man may drive the bride and groom to the reception. If he is not driving the bride and groom, the best man may stay behind and check that there are no stray guests in need of transportation to the reception.

At the reception, the best man mingles with the guests. If there is a sit-down meal, he is seated to the bride's right. He proposes the first toast to the bride and groom. They say a good toastmaster must be clever, be brief, and be seated. A toast may be humorous and sentimental, but it should always be in good taste. If the best man acts as master of ceremonies, he introduces the speakers and announces the first dance and the cutting of the wedding cake.

The best man dances with the bride after the groom, her father and/or stepfather, and her father-in-law have had their turns.

At the end of the reception, the best man helps the groom out of his wedding clothes. When the couple are ready to leave the reception, he escorts the groom's family to the dressing room to say good-bye. He then leads the couple past the assembled guests to the exit and escorts them to their car. He double-checks that the couple's luggage is in the car and may even drive them to their motel or to the airport. He may check the luggage and give the baggage claim checks to the groom. The best man may also make sure the groom has his traveler's checks, boat or plane tickets, car keys, and so on. If the couple are staying at a nearby hotel or motel, he may register for them and give the room key to the groom. After a job well done, he may return to the reception to relax and enjoy himself.

The Informal Wedding

For a small, private, wedding ceremony at home, in a church, or in a judge's chambers, the bride may ask only a maid or matron of honor to be her attendant and witness. Usually, this is either a sister or a close friend, whose dress or suit is in tune with the bride's attire. The groom may invite a best man to stand by his side and be his witness. This may be a brother, father, or best friend, whose attire matches that of the groom in formality.

The Semiformal Wedding

In addition to the maid or matron of honor and the best man, any number of bridesmaids and groomsmen may be invited to be part of the wedding party. The attendants are usually close in age, and it is perfectly correct to have married bridesmaids and groomsmen, even if their spouses are not included in the wedding party. However, spouses are asked to all wedding and rehearsal parties.

The boutonnieres for the groomsmen and the bouquets for the brides-maids should be waiting for them at the church before the wedding.

Bridesmaids

The bridesmaids are all close friends or relatives of the bride, and it is thoughtful—but not necessary—to include the groom's sister. She may be given another honored role. It is also possible to have two maids or matrons of honor who share responsibilities. One may be in charge of the groom's ring, and the other may help the bride with her veil and train. Bridesmaids have few duties to perform at the wedding except to add charm and beauty to the ceremony, to mingle cheerfully with the guests at the reception, and to be generally helpful.

Groomsmen and Ushers

The groomsmen are usually close friends and relatives of the groom, and the bride's brother is often included. A groomsman's responsibility is to attend the rehearsal and to arrive properly attired at the church forty-five minutes to one hour ahead of time.

At many weddings, groomsmen also act as ushers. For large weddings, or when the attendants include more men than women, some men may act as groomsmen while others act as ushers. Separate ushers wear the same attire as the groomsmen. Ushers seat the guests, who usually arrive about twenty minutes before the ceremony. For a small wedding there are usually two ushers; for larger weddings, a good rule of thumb is to have one usher for every fifty guests. One usher may be asked to act as head usher.

The ushers line up on the left side of the entrance. As the guests enter, one usher at a time steps forward and asks if they are friends of the bride or groom. The usher accompanies the bride's relatives and friends to their seats on the left side of the aisle and the groom's relatives and friends to the right side of the aisle. (In Orthodox synagogues, the seating is reversed.) At weddings where the great majority of guests are friends or relatives of one family, it is perfectly proper to seat guests on either side of the aisle to make the congregation look more balanced.

An usher offers his right arm to a female guest and escorts her down the aisle to her seat. If a man is accompanying a woman, he follows a step or two behind the usher and female guest. If two women arrive together, the usher escorts the elder woman down the aisle to her seat. Unaccompanied men simply walk with the usher to their seats. When many guests are waiting, one or two guests may walk down the aisle behind the usher and a guest he is escorting.

It is important for ushers to remember that the reserved front pews on each side of the center aisle are for the immediate family and close friends of the bride and groom. The people who sit here are either notified by word of mouth or given pew cards to be presented to the usher. Ushers may also be given a list of people to be seated in reserved pews in case guests forget their pew cards.

It is kind of ushers to exchange a few friendly remarks as they escort wedding guests to their seats. Any pleasant comment about the weather, mutual friends, or so on is fine. After guests are seated, one or two ushers roll out the white aisle runner if needed. The head usher then escorts the bride's mother to the front left pew. This is the signal to the congregation that the ceremony is about to begin. Tardy guests are not ushered to seats; rather, they occupy pews at the back.

If the ushers are also groomsmen, they then lead the processional as arranged at the rehearsal. After the ceremony, they take their designated place in the recessional, then return to the front pews and escort any unaccompanied women of the bride and groom's immediate families up the aisle.

For those acting as groomsmen only, their role at the ceremony is fulfilled when they escort the groom to the altar.

At the reception, both groomsmen and ushers can make themselves useful by introducing guests to one another, dancing with single women, keeping a friendly eye on youngsters, offering an umbrella if needed, or helping the photographer assemble subjects for group photographs. In addition, their help may be required in getting guests off to the airport or escorting bridesmaids to their homes when the reception is over.

The Formal Wedding

There are usually more attendants at a formal wedding, and these may include junior bridesmaids, a flower girl, a ring bearer, and pages (if the bride has a very long train). Ushers may also have more responsibilities at a formal wedding, such as removing the pew ribbons used to identify reserved seats. After guests are seated, the ribbons are replaced.

For a candlelight ceremony, two ushers light the candles, starting from the back of the church, about fifteen minutes before the ceremony. They slowly move down the aisle together, using tapers to light each candle on the left and right side of the aisle.

Children's Roles

It is becoming more and more common for children to be involved in the wedding ceremony. There are a number of ways they can be included, depending entirely on their disposition and age. Very young children (under the age of five) are unpredictable and ought not to be given important roles. Instead, they may be included in the wedding photographs and invited to have the first piece of wedding cake. Older children (under the age of ten) may be flower girls, ring bearers, or pages. Junior bridesmaids, junior groomsmen, and candle lighters may be over ten and into their early teens.

Child attendants are included in the rehearsal, but need not remain for the dinner or be included in prewedding parties. They are invited with their parents to the wedding reception.

Parents of young children involved in the wedding are seated in one of the front pews on the aisle. The little ones may sit with their parents after walking down the aisle, since it would be difficult for them to stand without fidgeting during the entire ceremony.

If there are numerous children involved in the wedding, it may be wise to assign a relative or hire a babysitter or kindergarten teacher to supervise the young attendants at the reception. A children's table may be set up for them, and gifts of coloring books, crayons, and small toys may be provided to keep everyone happy.

Children's Roles in a Second Marriage

Parents have several choices when it comes to including their children both during the ceremony and the reception. Much depends on the age of the son or daughter. Grown children may be asked to serve as witnesses and take on the responsibilities of best man or maid or matron of honor. For an informal wedding, they may simply be asked to stand up with their parents. They may recite readings during the ceremony or give toasts at the reception. A silver-framed family photograph with the date engraved on it will surely be a treasured gift.

Teenagers may also be asked to stand up with their parents as bridesmaids or groomsmen. The formality of having someone "give away" the bride should be overlooked. In many states a legal witness must be eighteen or older; therefore, a teenager is not eligible to act as maid of honor or best man. The clergyperson may mention a son or daughter by name during the ceremony and may present a medallion, pendant, or locket with the date as a memento of the occasion. Teenage children may be asked to hand out programs, act as ushers, or light candles.

A young child may be a flower girl, ring bearer, or page at a formal wedding. At an informal wedding, a young child may walk down the aisle with his or her parent and sit in one of the front pews with relatives during the ceremony. Young children of the bride or groom are included in wedding pictures, and during the reception they may be served the first piece of wedding cake.

The Flower Girl

The flower girl walks in just ahead of the bride alone, with the ring bearer, or with another flower girl of about the same height. She wears a party dress and ballet slippers or patent-leather shoes. Traditionally, she scattered rose petals in the bride's path, but since this is now considered to be slippery and dangerous, it is more common today for her to carry a flower basket or a tiny nosegay.

The Ring Bearer

The ring bearer precedes or walks with the flower girl. The child balances a white lace or satin pillow on his hands. A dummy bride's ring is tied to the center with ribbons or stitched lightly with a white thread. For a double-ring ceremony, a second ring bearer might carry a pillow with the groom's ring attached. The adult attendants keep the genuine rings safe.

The ring bearer may wear either a dark blue blazer with knee pants or a satin or velvet suit. If he resists wearing a bow tie or cummerbund, do not insist on it.

Pages or Train Bearers

Pages are needed only when the bride has a very long train. They usually walk side-by-side behind the bride and are about the same height.

Junior Groomsmen, Junior Bridesmaids, and Candle Lighters

These boys and girls always add special warmth to a wedding. Junior groomsmen and bridesmaids perform the same duties as adult groomsmen and bridesmaids. The duty of the candle lighter is to step forward and light the candles at the altar just before the mother of the bride is seated. After the recession, as guests leave the sanctuary, they return and extinguish the candles.

Pets

This question has been put to me recently: "Our dog is like a member of the family; how can he be included in the wedding?" My answer is to include your pet in your cherished wedding photographs, which will be long treasured by you and your family.

Notes

Notes

Chapter Nine

What to Wear

Something old, something new,
Something borrowed, something blue.

ANONYMOUS

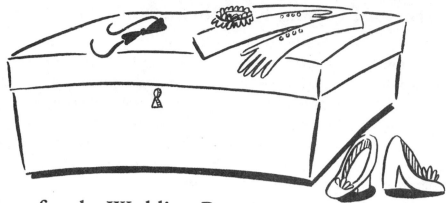

Dress for the Wedding Party

Before the bride and groom have the pleasure of selecting their attire, they first must decide the level of formality of their wedding. They must also decide on the time of day and the season. These decisions dictate the style, fabric, and color of the bride's gown; the length of her skirt; and whether she will wear a veil or headpiece. Formality, time, and season also dictate what the men in the wedding party will wear.

It is best if the bride and groom discuss their dress preferences before going shopping. Then they will be in a much better position to choose attire that will create a pleasing total effect for the entire wedding party and a cherished group photograph.

Dressing in Harmony

What the bride and groom decide to wear is entirely up to them, of course, but they ought to be dressed in harmony with each other and with the rest of the wedding party. If the bride wishes to wear a formal wedding gown with a veil, she must be sure that the groom is willing to dress formally as well. The same holds true for bridesmaids and groomsmen.

If an attendant has financial difficulties, this should be discussed openly. The bride and groom may offer to subsidize the rental of a suit or the purchase of a gown and shoes, or the attendant may graciously decline the honor of serving in the wedding party.

Terms Describing Formality

The words used to describe formality of dress—"casual," "informal," "semiformal," and "formal"—on invitations must be clearly defined, because there is still a great deal of confusion regarding these terms in all parts of the country and among all segments of society! It becomes especially bewildering when people who live in different communities or regions of the country compare notes by telephone. The only way for guests to know for sure what is expected of them is for the host to state what should be worn clearly on the invitation.

Here is a true—though extreme—story that illustrates the above point: A couple visiting in Bermuda were invited to a wedding. They called ahead and asked what to wear and were told the wedding was informal. The man wore a blue suit, white shirt, and patterned tie. Much to his chagrin, he saw upon arriving at the wedding that all the other male guests were wearing tuxedos. The dinner jacket was considered informal in this community, and the cutaway suit with white tie was considered formal.

In the U.S., the word "informal" or "casual" can mean anything from tennis shoes and a parka for the young to Gucci loafers and a camel-hair sports coat without a tie for the older set. In this book, the words "informal" and "casual" are not addressed. We will not concern ourselves with what shoes to wear for a wedding on the beach or what to wear if the wedding party will ride to the ceremony on motorcycles.

Today "elegant casual" may be considered equivalent to "semiformal." Elegant casual or semiformal dress for women means a dressy dress or pantsuit, and for men means a suit and tie. Invitations sometimes come right out and say "suit and tie."

Sometimes invitations say "black tie optional." This means that if a man owns a tuxedo, he should wear it; if he does not own one, he needn't rent one. For a woman, it means a cocktail dress. "Formal" means white tie for men and usually long gowns for women. "Summer formal" means white jackets for the men, with colorful cummerbunds and bow ties.

The Wedding Gown

It is a relief to know that the bride has innumerable choices. She can buy a dress off the rack and have it altered to fit, or given enough time, she can custom-order a gown from a bridal salon. She may decide to wear her mother's wedding gown or a treasured family heirloom. She may borrow a gown or even rent one, which is just as practical nowadays for the bride as for the groom, who often rents his suit. The bride may prefer to wear an outfit from her homeland, such as an Indian sari, a Mexican wedding dress, or a Japanese kimono. She can lovingly sew her own gown or have a talented dressmaker design one for her.

There are several books available that give explicit directions with diagrams on how to sew your own wedding dress. One written by Gail Brown and Karen Dillon and published by Palmer/Pletsch Associates is titled *Sew a Beautiful Wedding Dress*.

Some large fabric stores not only have a wide selection of beautiful fabrics, along with both imported and domestic laces, they also have the names of reliable dressmakers they are willing to recommend. Some may be members of the Professional Association of Custom Clothiers (PACC). You may inquire about dressmakers yourself by writing to PACC, P.O. Box 8071, Medford, Oregon 97504-0071 or by calling 541-772-4119. You may also locate a local chapter by visiting the PACC website at www.paccprofessionals.org.

One experienced seamstress explained to me that she typically combines two or three dress patterns to create a unique dress to suit a particular bride. If the bride is living in a different city—away at school, for instance—the seamstress makes up a muslin sample and mails it to the bride for fitting. The result is a fashionable original at a fraction of the cost of a designer dress purchased in a fine store.

As for color, the bride may choose any color that suits her fancy. In the United States, brides usually wear white, ivory, or pastel. (This isn't necessarily so in other countries—for example, in China, brides wear red, and in Norway, brides wear green!) Every spring and fall, bridal salons receive new styles that reflect current fashions. Shopping for clothes for the bride and her attendants should begin at least six months before the wedding for special orders. This allows time for fittings and newspaper photographs.

Many large department stores put on extravagant bridal fashion shows with up-to-the-minute styles. Attending these shows is one way to size up what is available for the entire wedding party in colors, fabrics, and designs. Attending a bridal show often helps a bride decide not only what she likes, but also what she dislikes.

When the bride is ready to begin shopping for her gown, she might go with her mother or a trusted friend who can help her narrow down her choices. Shopping with too many people will only be confusing.

After looking around at several bridal salons, it is best for the bride to make an appointment with the salon of her choice. She should talk frankly and openly with the salesperson about her requirements and spending limit. Because most salespeople work on commission, they often begin by showing their most expensive lines first. It is terribly hard for a bride to resist the temptation of buying a dream dress that is beyond her means. It is better to select two or three favorites and then return to see the dresses again before making a final selection.

If the bride is buying a gown to match an heirloom veil, she should bring the veil to the salon to aid in making a perfect match in color and design.

The Pregnant Bride

Bridal salons do not advertise their special lines of wedding gowns for pregnant brides, but they do carry them! A pregnant bride should advise her fitter of the pregnancy during her first appointment. This will save extra alterations on the final fitting and will be much appreciated by the fitter.

The Second Time Around

What a bride wears the second time around depends greatly on her age and the circumstances of her first wedding. Let's consider a very young woman who eloped and whose marriage may have been annulled. In her case, there's no reason she could not enjoy a truly formal wedding with all the trimmings. Now let's consider a woman who had an enormous church wedding with hundreds of guests a few years ago. When she remarries, it is in far better taste for her to invite a few close friends to a private ceremony followed by a reception. What about a widow who was happily married for many years and now has grown children and grandchildren? Everyone is delighted at the prospect of her marriage. A lovely semiformal wedding is certainly appropriate in her case. She might choose a dressy off-white or pastel gown of midcalf length without a train.

A second-time bride typically does not wear a veil, as a veil is a traditional symbol of being young and virginal. Instead, a second-time bride may wear a hair ornament, a flower, or a small hat.

Preserving the Gown

The bride should arrange for someone to take her gown to a reputable dry cleaner after the wedding. Some cleaners will also pack the gown in an airtight box. This process, which is costly, preserves the gown so that it may be worn again on a special anniversary or kept for future wear by other members of the family. If a bride chooses to have her gown preserved in this way, she should insist on inspecting the gown before it is sealed in the box.

The Train

The length of the train does not determine the formality of the wedding. There are various types of trains, including the cathedral train, which is three to six yards long; the chapel train, which is very full and is eight to twelve inches long; and the sweep train, which is part of the dress and barely sweeps the floor.

The Veil

Veils are available in a variety of designs. A veil may flow to the shoulder, elbow, fingertips, ankles, or floor. A shorter veil is lovely when the detail on the back of the dress is particularly interesting. A longer veil may work well with a very formal gown. It is up to the bride to decide what length and style of veil best complements her gown. Sometimes a long, delicate veil may double as a train while permitting the design of the dress to show through.

A veil may be held in place with a circlet of pearls or flowers, a decorative headband or comb, by hairpins concealed in a tiny bunch of fresh flowers, or by a tiara. A blusher may be attached to a longer veil and worn over the face and headpiece. A birdcage veil falls below the chin and may be attached to a hat. A flyaway veil consists of several layers brushing the shoulders.

Gloves for the Bride

When her dress has no sleeves or short sleeves, the bride may decide to wear long gloves. With three-quarter sleeves, she may prefer to wear short gloves. During the ring ceremony, the bride may remove a short glove from her left hand and give it to the maid of honor. If she is wearing long gloves, the underseam of the ring finger may be slit so that the top can be folded back in order for her finger to receive the ring. If the gloves have buttons at the wrist, the entire hand of the glove may be tucked under, above the wrist. The engagement ring may be transferred to the right hand and worn under the glove.

Although the bride may wear gloves in the receiving line and at the reception, she never eats with gloves on.

Hairstyles

Some brides like to do their own hair and wear it naturally. Other brides prefer to do something special on this memorable day. If the bride plans to have her hair styled at a posh beauty salon, she should make an appointment well in advance. It is wise to let the stylist do a trial run once before the wedding to get the feel of the thickness and texture of the bride's hair, and to allow the bride to approve the hairstyle. If the bride will be wearing a veil, she should bring it to the salon so her hair can be suitably styled. The stylist will also want to know the lines of the dress—especially the neckline and sleeves—in order to create an elegant head-to-toe look.

A bride may prefer to wear fresh flowers and/or ribbons twined in a braid instead of a veil. In this case, it is wise to choose hardy flowers. Some long-lasting flowers are rosebuds, miniature carnations, gardenias, statice, and daisies. Baby's breath is also very appealing, because it creates a delicate halo that trembles when the bride moves. One can also combine real baby's breath with silk flowers.

If the bridesmaids have hair of similar length and all are agreeable, they might all wear their hair in the same graceful style, either loose or up in a chignon or twist. It may be more convenient in this case to have a hairdresser come to one's home and arrange everyone's hair before the wedding.

Bride's Attendants

It is the bride's privilege to choose the design, the material, and the color of her attendants' dresses to complement her own. The gowns may be purchased in a bridal salon, or the bride may supply the name of a dressmaker who will make all the dresses for the wedding party. The bride may also provide patterns for the bridesmaids. For a small, informal wedding with one or two attendants, the bride may approve of outfits that the women already own.

For a larger wedding, the selection of gowns for the bridesmaids and the maid or matron of honor needs special care. It is usually best to select new gowns for these attendants to purchase so that all the gowns will complement each other. The bride should consider how the gown will look on each attendant, not only in terms of style and color, but also for her age. A dress that is charming on an eighteen-year-old might make a bridesmaid over thirty feel silly. And since the bridesmaids pay for their own dresses, it is considerate to select a style that is within each bridesmaid's budget and that may be worn again after the wedding. If a bridesmaid encounters financial difficulty, the bride may offer to pay for the dress as a gift to the bridesmaid. This matter is kept confidential, of course, unless the bride offers to purchase dresses for all the bridesmaids.

The maid or matron of honor's dress is usually the same style as the bridesmaids' dresses, but a different color. Her gown may be a deeper tone, or her dress and bouquet may use colors in reverse of those of the bridesmaids.

Simply having attendants wear white, silver, or gold slippers instead of dying shoes to match their gowns saves a lot of time, trouble, and money. If shoes are to be dyed, they should all be done in one store in order to match exactly. If the bridesmaids live in different cities, they may either buy their shoes and mail them to the bride for dyeing or shop at the same chain store and select their shoes and dye color by number.

Junior Bridesmaids, Flower Girls, and Ring Bearers

The parents of young attendants pay for the purchase or rental of the outfits worn by their children.

A junior bridesmaid may wear a gown suitable for her age and similar in design, color, and fabric to the gowns of the other bridesmaids.

A flower girl's dress should be suitable to her age in style (usually a pinafore or a dress with a sash) and should harmonize with the bridesmaids' gowns in color and fabric.

A ring bearer may wear any color suit—dark in the winter and light in the summer. Short pants with knee socks are preferred for a very young boy. An older boy may wear a traditional suit or blazer and a boutonniere to match those of the groomsmen.

The most important point to remember in selecting clothing for young people is that they often grow unexpectedly and rapidly. It's best not to have any final fittings until just prior to the wedding.

Mothers of the Bride and Groom

The dresses of the bride and groom's mothers should blend with the attire of the rest of the wedding party. The bride's mother usually selects her dress first and notifies the groom's mother of the color and style. The mothers should choose dresses that are becoming on them and that suit their tastes, so they may wear the dresses happily on future occasions. In the past, the mothers were restricted only from wearing black or white. Black was considered the color for mourning, and white was reserved for the bride. Lately, however, even this long-standing tradition has fallen by the wayside!

Fathers of the Bride and Groom

The bride and groom's fathers should wear the same attire as the groom and his attendants, especially if they will be walking down the aisle and/or standing in the receiving line. Matching outfits also look better in the keepsake photographs.

If a father will not be walking down the aisle, standing in the receiving line, or otherwise participating in the wedding party, he may wear the same sort of suit that male guests will be wearing.

Purchasing a Tuxedo

When a man attends a black-tie affair, he should feel comfortable and at ease. Owning your own tuxedo is an advantage if you attend formal affairs more than once or twice a year. It is convenient and time-saving to own a tuxedo that fits and is readily accessible. And, of course, you save on recurring rental fees.

A rental tuxedo often has a strong, thick nylon lining that can withstand numerous dry cleanings, an expandable waistband, and telescopic sleeves that allow for adjustments. Such a tuxedo can never fit as well or be as comfortable as one that has been made to measure or purchased in a fine men's store.

In selecting a tuxedo, some good rules of thumb are as follows: (1) For a long-term investment, do not buy anything faddish. (2) Shop in about the same price range as you are accustomed to paying for a business suit. (3) Wool tuxedos are preferable because wool breathes better and wrinkles less than other fabrics. Blends of 45 percent wool and 55 percent polyester are also good. Tropical-weight wool, which can be worn year-round, is the best investment. (4) The style of a tuxedo should be conservative and the

Dear Edith,

I would like to wear a traditional long wedding gown and veil to my church wedding, but my fiancé does not want to wear a tuxedo. Is it all right for the groomsmen to wear tuxedos if the groom wears a business suit?

ANSWER: Not really! Everyone in the wedding party should be dressed in a complementary style. It makes for a much better picture when everyone is dressed in harmony. If the bride wears a formal wedding gown, the groom should also wear a formal suit—such as a stroller, tuxedo, or tails— depending on the time of day the wedding takes place. If the bride wears a semiformal dress, then the groom may wear a suit. If the bride and groom cannot agree on what they will wear to their wedding—if they are not willing to compromise to please each other—then they may want to take a closer look at their compatibility.

SEMIFORMAL
DAY WEDDING

Oxford gray stroller coat worn
with striped trousers; gray
double-breasted waistcoat;
four-in-hand tie with turn-
down collar; plain-toe black
shoes; gray suede or mocha
gloves; black or gray Homburg;
pearl stick pin; gold, pearl, or
stone studs and links.

FORMAL
DAY WEDDING

Oxford gray cutaway worn with
gray double-breasted waistcoat;
striped trousers; silk ascot with
wing collar or four-in-hand with
turn-down collar; plain-toe black
shoes; gray suede gloves; silk
top hat; pearl stick pin; gold,
pearl, or stone links and studs.

SEMIFORMAL EVENING
WEDDING

Tuxedo worn with white pleated
or piqué-front shirt with turn-
down collar; black or midnight
blue bow tie with matching
cummerbund; black shoes;
Homburg, gray suede gloves,
if desired.

FORMAL EVENING WEDDING

Full-dress tuxedo worn with matching white piqué
shirt; waistcoat; bow tie and wing collar; plain-toe
black shoes; white gloves; white studs and links.

SUMMER EVENING WEDDING

White dinner jacket worn with black or midnight blue
trousers; black or midnight blue cummerbund and
matching bow tie; black pumps or oxfords; white
pleated or piqué-front shirt with turn-down collar;
lightweight straw hat; gold or pearl studs and links.

color black so it won't go out of style. You can add variety by wearing a printed or a colored matching tie and cummerbund (instead of the traditional black tie and cummerbund) or by wearing a shirt of a unique design.

Men's Formal Rental Clothing

With our casual lifestyle today, few men own tuxedos or formal dress suits, yet they still occasionally need to dress formally—often for weddings. Wedding parties look much more attractive and uniform when all the men are dressed alike for the ceremony and the pictures. Rental stores allow men to avoid purchasing clothing they will seldom wear, and they give brides and grooms a much greater selection of styles and colors for any time of year.

There are numerous places—some more fashionable than others— where one can rent a wide selection of men's clothing: coats, trousers, shirts, vests, ties, ascots, cummerbunds, shoes . . . everything except underwear and socks! Before visiting a men's rental store, you may want to check

Dear Edith,
I've been shopping around for men's rental tuxedos. How can I tell where I can get the best deal?

ANSWER: Prices vary according to geographic location and volume turnover. Of major importance: Does the rental store provide minor fittings and alterations? A man can feel extremely uncomfortable and ill at ease when he is tripping over his trouser legs or when the edge of his sleeve reaches his knuckles instead of his wrist.

A man should be professionally measured for a good fit across the shoulders so there is no pull across the back of the jacket. Also, one must be sure there is no gap between the trousers and the vest, if a vest is called for.

Men may be fitted in any good men's clothing store and the measurements recorded on a form. The goal is to have the suit look as if it were tailor-made, not rented.

out current trends on the world wide web, in bridal magazines, or at a bridal show. Then head to a rental store in the city where the wedding will take place and select the style you like best.

If any of the men in the wedding party live near the store you've selected, they should be measured at that store. Men who live far away should be measured in good men's stores in the cities where they live.

Measurements are required for the chest, waist, height, trouser inseam, shirt size, and sleeve inseam. Only an experienced fitter knows how to take these measurements correctly. For example, when measuring an athlete with large thighs and calves and a slim waist, an experienced fitter knows that it is far better to order a larger size trouser and take a tuck in the waist than to order trousers according to a waist measurement, which may cause binding in the legs.

Each male attendant should obtain a form listing his correct measurements. He should then mail the form to whoever is responsible for ordering the rental attire. This responsible person takes all the forms to the chosen rental store and orders the necessary suits, shoes, and so on. Ideally, the men in the wedding party will visit this store to be fitted a few days prior to the wedding. They may, for instance, be fitted on a Thursday, have their alterations done on Friday, and pick up their suits on Saturday, the day of the wedding.

Different rental stores carry different brands and qualities of formalwear, so prices will vary from store to store. Some provide alteration services, and some do not. As always, it is wise to check around before committing oneself.

Elements of Men's Formalwear

In the sections that follow, you'll find tips regarding the various elements of men's formalwear. Please note that traditionally, tuxedos are not worn in the daytime. An Oxford gray stroller with a high-button vest and striped trousers is recommended for a semiformal wedding in the morning. An Oxford gray cutaway is recommended for a formal wedding in the afternoon before six o'clock.

The rule described above is not always observed, however. By the same token, dress rules for formal weddings are also frequently bent. The white tie and tails are rarely worn—even for the most formal weddings.

Tuxedo

You may choose a single-breasted, shawl-collar tuxedo or a double-breasted, notched-collar, two-button tuxedo. Your choice depends somewhat on your figure. An associate at a men's store can help you determine the style that looks best on you.

Shirt

The pleated shirt with banded collar is the most popular shirt style. The sleeve may show one to one-and-a-half inches below the sleeve of the jacket.

Bow Tie

Rental stores offer pretied bow ties; however, tying your own tie is as simple as tying your shoelace, and it looks sharper. (You can practice by tying one around your knee before you attempt to tie one around your neck.) When you're ready, place the tie around your neck with both ends hanging down. Do not look in a mirror; it will only confuse you. Then tie a conventional bow. After you have tied the bow, you can check how it looks in the mirror.

I recently attended a wedding where the groom decided he would wear a white tie instead of a black tie with his tuxedo. It was a novel idea—and most becoming.

Suspenders

Although there are several built-in adjustments in rental suits, some rental stores provide gray or black-and-white suspenders. Suspenders can help prevent trousers from slipping below the vest, which reveals a band of the white shirt and detracts from a trim appearance.

Vest

The vest is a prominent accessory in the tuxedo rental service. High, six-button Edwardian vests are currently very popular. They may be white or may match the colors of the bridesmaids' dresses.

Cummerbund

A cummerbund is worn when a vest is not. This band around the waist is worn pleats-up and may be of any color or fabric. It usually matches the tie.

Ascot

An ascot is a broad neck scarf knotted so that one end lies flat over the other. When the men in the wedding party own their own formalwear, the groom selects ascots and sends an identical one to each man as a gift.

Gloves

At an informal wedding, none of the men wear gloves. At a formal wedding, groomsmen always wear gloves, although the groom and best man may not. If the groom and best man do wear gloves, the groom hands his gloves to the best man before the ceremony, and the best man tucks both pairs of gloves into his own pocket.

Studs and Cuff Links

Studs take the place of buttons on a shirt front, and cuff links take the place of buttons on a shirtsleeve. If a man does not own his own studs and cuff links, they are widely available for rent with dress shirts.

Shoes

Nowadays, some men own nothing but a pair of loafers and and a pair of tennis shoes. Fortunately, patent leather dress shoes are also available to rent in most stores.

Dress for the Informal Wedding

An informal wedding may take place at home, in a city hall, in a clergymember's study, in a friend's home, at a club, or in any congenial setting. The ceremony guest list may be restricted to close relatives and friends, or in the case of a second marriage, may include the children of the bride and/or groom. The ceremony may be followed by a reception to which additional friends are invited.

In the daytime, the bride and her attendants may wear dressy suits or short cocktail dresses. The groom may wear a dark suit and tie in the winter. He may wear a light suit and tie, or a navy jacket with white or khaki trousers, in the summer. In hot climates, he may choose a white or beige suit.

After six o'clock, the bride may choose to wear a long dress, in which case the groom and his attendants wear dark suits in the winter, light suits in the summer, or tuxedos.

Dress for the Semiformal Wedding

When the wedding takes place at home, in a church, or in a private club, hotel, or public facility, the bride wears a long wedding gown (veil optional) for both daytime and evening. Her attendants may wear any fashionable-length bridesmaid gowns.

Before six o'clock, the groom and his attendants wear a sack coat or stroller with black-and-gray striped trousers, gray vest, white shirt with turn-down collar and four-in-hand tie, and black smooth-toe shoes with black socks. Gray gloves and a black or gray Homburg are optional.

After six o'clock, the groom and his attendants wear black tuxedos in the winter. A white or cream jacket with a pleated or piqué soft shirt, cummerbund, black or midnight blue bow tie, and black patent leather or kid shoes are worn in the summer. Gray suede gloves are optional.

The Most Formal Wedding

Before or after six o'clock, the bride and her attendants all wear ankle-length or long gowns. The bride's dress has a train, and her veil may be of any length.

The mothers of the bride and groom may wear short or long dresses in the daytime. They usually wear long dresses or short cocktail dresses in the evening.

Before six o'clock, the groom and his attendants wear what is called a morning coat or cutaway, striped trousers, vest, shirt with winged collar, and a silk ascot or gray-and-black striped four-in-hand tie. Black silk socks, black kid shoes, top hat, and gray gloves are optional.

After six o'clock, the groom and attendants wear full-dress black tail coats and trousers, white bow ties, white gloves, black silk socks, and black patent leather shoes or pumps. Top hats are optional. Alternatively, the groomsmen may wear matching tuxedos. In the summer, all the men in the wedding party may wear dinner jackets instead of tails.

The Military Wedding

The military wedding is like any other wedding, except the groom and his attendants are in uniform, and they do not wear boutonnieres. The style of uniform depends on the hour of ceremony, the type of wedding, and the season. Dress blues or whites are worn during the day and for informal weddings. In the evening, the mess uniform is worn, and for very formal evening weddings, the evening dress uniform is worn.

Notes

Notes

Chapter Ten

Flowers

My love is like a red red rose
That's newly sprung in June;
Oh, my love is like the melody
That's sweetly played in tune.

ROBERT BURNS

Since time immemorial, flowers have added beauty, fragrance, and distinction to weddings. Flowers can, with a little imagination, be cost-controlled in several ways: (1) Select flowers in season from a florist whose work you like; (2) Look around for nonprofessional help; (3) Combine professional and nonprofessional help; (4) Consider sharing expenses with another couple who are having a wedding on the same day in the same place.

The one thing that no couple should attempt is to arrange flowers themselves for a large wedding and/or reception.

Flowers in Season

Flowers in season are usually the least costly option. Easter lilies, white tulips, and lilacs are traditional in early spring. White peonies frequently bloom in May. Roses bloom throughout the summer. White daisies combined with fern, baby's breath, or Queen Anne's lace also make a charming summer arrangement. In fall and winter, a variety of white chrysanthemums and poinsettias are readily available.

The Professional Florist

It is a good idea to make an appointment with a florist or a floral designer who specializes in weddings. Arranging flowers for weddings is a time-consuming and exacting job; therefore, it is important to select a florist who has had experience with all the detailed planning that goes along with a wedding. The ideal florist is artistic, patient, reliable, and experienced. The florist must be willing to spend adequate time consulting with the bride and groom. (When a couple are unsure of what flowers to select, one experienced florist I know says, "Tell me what flowers you don't like!") Special orders require special attention, and deliveries must be punctual. Be sure to give your florist detailed instructions regarding the time and place of delivery.

It is helpful if the florist is familiar with the church or reception site, because he or she must be aware of the lighting and layout of the area. If the florist is unfamiliar with the wedding site, be sure he or she visits the place well in advance of your wedding.

When you reach an agreement on the kind, amount, placement, price, and delivery of flowers, confirm all arrangements with your florist in writing, either by letter or by contract. The florist may require a deposit, but under no circumstances should the total fee be paid before the day of your wedding. Appoint someone to see that the flowers are correct, delivered on time, and arranged properly on your wedding day.

Nonprofessional Help

If your wedding will take place in a warm climate where flowers grow year-round or in the northern half of the United States during the spring or summer months, you may consider decorating artistically with fresh-cut flowers, flowering shrubs gathered from a country garden, or flowers gathered in the fields. With a bit of luck, a member of your local garden club may offer help, or you may enlist the help of a neighbor or friend whose passion is gardening. Someone who knows flowers well can be a marvelous source of useful information.

You may combine all your flowers—bouquets, corsages, boutonnieres, ceremony décor, and reception décor—into one order from your florist, but this is likely to be costly. If you can find a friend or relative to tastefully arrange table centerpieces at the reception, this can cut costs enormously. You might also designate someone to unobtrusively transport flowers from the ceremony to the reception site and have the bridesmaids place their flowers in a designated flower holder on the bridal table. This gives the attendants a place to put their flowers, and it also enhances the appearance of the table.

Flowers in a Church or Synagogue

There may be some regulations regarding use of flowers in your church or synagogue, so it is vital that you consult your clergymember, or whoever is in charge of wedding arrangements, before making any decisions.

Next, consider the lighting. Will it be a daytime or nighttime wedding? If the church interior is dimly lit, deep blue or lavender flowers will be lost in the shadows, while white or pastel flowers will stand out nicely. It is wise to focus your attention on the altar. Here, a few well-placed potted plants or individual flower arrangements often will do. Generally speaking, a large church with a high ceiling needs many tall flower arrangements if the flowers are to make any impact at all. Even in a small church, flowers must be visible from a distance; therefore, bold arrangements show up better than small, delicate blossoms.

For an elaborate wedding, flowers or ribbons may be draped down the aisle to mark the pews reserved for family members. Other options are to place greens or flowering sprays at strategic points. For an evening wedding, you might place candles surrounded by greens in the windows.

You may wish to place a large welcoming arrangement at the entrance or in the foyer, but this is not vital. Remember that when the bridesmaids walk down the aisle in colorful dresses and carrying lovely bouquets, all eyes are focused on them. It is far better to decorate the reception site with flowers and table centerpieces than to fill the church with massive flower arrangements. Everyone will spend more time at the reception, and flowers, like music, add to the atmosphere of gaiety and fun.

The Huppah

A huppah is a flowered canopy or arch used in Jewish wedding ceremonies. It must be large enough to cover the rabbi and the immediate wedding party. It symbolizes the home the bride and groom will share.

For a Very Small Wedding

If you will be holding a small wedding in a large church, you may be concerned about a sense of emptiness. You can overcome this by using the choir stalls in the chancel for guest seating and by lighting only this section of the church. You may also define the perimeter of the ceremony with a hedge of potted plants or a row of greenery. Finally you may consider renting small trees or decorating a trellis or screen to create a feeling of warmth and intimacy.

The Aisle Runner

A white aisle runner is usually available through your florist. Some people feel a runner is necessary only on grass, but this is a purely personal decision. For example, at past White House weddings, aisle runners were not used because it was felt the gowns photographed better without them.

Flowers in a Private Indoor Setting

At a home, in a club, or at a hotel, a room with a fireplace creates an ideal setting for a wedding ceremony. A fireplace may be filled with greens or plants, or the mantel may be decorated with a green garland or a flower arrangement. Most florists and rental stores have stands for flowers, potted plants, or candles, as well as arches, stanchions, and kneelers.

A bay window is also a lovely setting for the ceremony, but one must be sure that no bright light will glare in the window during the ceremony. If the scene outside the window is too bright, the guests will see the bride and groom as mere silhouettes. If no fireplace or bay window is available, a decorative screen or arrangement of greenery or flowers may be placed against a wall as a backdrop for the ceremony. In the evening, closed draperies make a soft, attractive backdrop.

Flowers in a Private Outdoor Setting

When the ceremony takes place in a garden, on a patio, under a tent, or by a pool, one can create many beautiful touches to enhance the setting.

For added color and lushness, potted plants may be stashed among flowerbeds or greenery or on a patio. Flowers and candles may also be floated in a pool. And, of course, arches or standards decorated with flowers may be placed in the designated ceremony area. Under a tent, branches or flowering twigs may be attached to the tent posts for a dramatic effect. A friendly florist may be asked about renting out potted plants for a few hours.

Other Outdoor Decorations

Silver or gold helium-filled balloons with the name of the couple and their wedding date make sensational centerpieces or accents for an outdoor wedding. A cluster or arch of balloons may be tied with colorful ribbons to create a lively entrance.

Floral Centerpieces at the Reception

Floral centerpieces at the reception may be as simple or elaborate as your budget permits. You might accent a Scotch theme with sprigs of heather or reflect the winter holidays with nuts, berries, and pine boughs. You might choose to provide breakaway centerpieces so that each guest can take home a small potted plant or bud vase as a favor.

Centerpieces ought to be low enough so guests can chat easily across the table. Alternatively, they should be tall and slim enough so that guests can easily see around them. In a room with a high ceiling, for example, you might use tall, clear glass columns filled with long-stemmed flowers that spray outward gracefully above eye level.

It is a good idea to decide in advance what to do with the centerpieces after the reception. Some may be given to hospitals or nursing homes, or one can make a list naming the special guests who should receive them. Discuss your plan with your florist and assign someone special to handle this chore.

Flowers for Members of the Wedding Party

When local custom requires it, the groom is responsible for purchasing the bride's bouquet and going-away corsage. The going-away corsage may be incorporated within the bridal bouquet or supplied separately. The groom may also be expected to pay for corsages for members of one or both families, although corsages are no longer mandatory. If used, the trend is to keep corsages simple so they may be worn at the shoulder or waistline, in the hair, on the wrist, or attached to a purse.

Often, however, the bride and groom simply combine all wedding-party flowers into one florist's order. The flowers should complement the bride's gown and her attendants' dresses.

A list of flowers for the wedding party might include the following:

1. The bride's bouquet and going-away corsage
2. Bouquets for female attendants
3. Corsages for the bride and groom's mothers and grandmothers
4. Boutonnieres for the groom, male attendants, and bride and groom's fathers and grandfathers
5. Corsages or boutonnieres for any special guests or people performing special wedding duties

The Bridal Bouquet

As the bride walks down the aisle, the flowers she carries accent the head-to-toe effect of her outfit. For example, if the gown has intricate detail in front, it is best if the bride carries a large single flower or simple bouquet. If, however, the gown has simple lines in front, the bride may prefer a more elaborate bouquet. Be sure to describe the bride's gown in detail for the florist. If the bride will be wearing an old-fashioned wedding gown, the florist may recommend that she carry an old-fashioned or Victorian bouquet—probably one including sweetheart roses, cornflowers, miniature carnations, and baby's breath. Or the florist may suggest a dried or silk arrangement with a lace collar. In some cases, the bride may wish to carry a small family Bible or a satin purse with a flower pinned to it.

For a very formal wedding in which the bride will wear a long gown, she may choose a cascade arrangement of all-white stephanotis and lilies of the valley. The bouquet may be made up of a single kind of flower or a combination of several kinds. Another option—particularly effective for the tall bride—is an arrangement of calla lilies. Smaller brides will prefer more delicate arrangements. The bride should also consider the texture of her gown when choosing her flowers. Eyelet and cotton are best complemented by daisies and violets. Camellias and gardenias, with their shiny dark leaves, are beautiful against a satin or brocade dress.

Surprisingly, bridesmaids' flowers are often more eye-catching than the bridal bouquet because it is the bride's dress—not her flowers—that is the focus of attention.

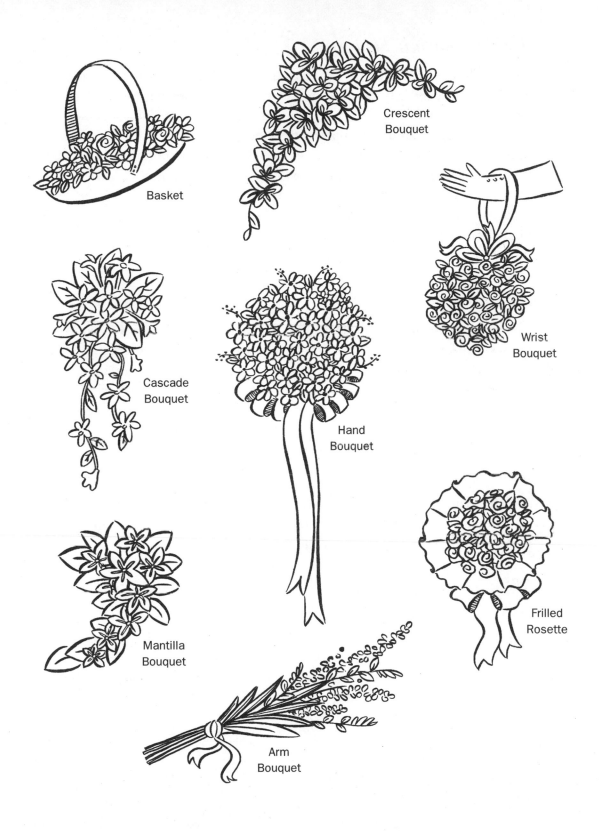

Basket

Crescent
Bouquet

Wrist
Bouquet

Cascade
Bouquet

Hand
Bouquet

Frilled
Rosette

Mantilla
Bouquet

Arm
Bouquet

The Bridesmaids' Flowers

The flowers carried by the bridesmaids should be coordinated with the bride's bouquet. Each bridesmaid may carry a basket filled with an arrangement of multicolored flowers, a nosegay, an arm bouquet of long-stemmed roses or chrysanthemums wrapped with ribbon; a Victorian tussie-mussie (a small, cone-shaped, hand-held container), a fan, a parasol, dried flowers, fresh greens mixed with a few garden-variety flowers, or a muff fashioned from flowers or fur with a floral accent. In short, just about anything the bride might select is suitable to carry out the theme of her wedding. At one lovely wedding I attended in Hawaii, everyone in the wedding party wore a flower lei.

Headdresses

Brides, bridesmaids, and flower girls sometimes wear flowers as head-dresses. (In Austria, for example, brides wear wreaths of fresh myrtle, which is considered a symbol of love.) Flowers formed into a crown or a tiara may be used with a wedding veil, or a combination of orange blossoms and ribbons is lovely. Flowers used in a headdress must look delicate but be sturdy enough to remain fresh and intact throughout the wedding.

Maid or Matron of Honor

The maid or matron of honor's bouquet is usually similar in style to the bridesmaids' bouquets, but different in color. This distinction helps the guests identify members of the wedding party.

The Groom, Groomsmen, Ushers, and Fathers

A boutonniere consists of a single blossom, such as a carnation or rosebud, or a shaft of tiny blooms such as lilies of the valley, and is quite often white. A boutonniere is worn on the left lapel. The groom's boutonniere complements the bride's bouquet and is a little different from those of the groomsmen, ushers, and fathers, whose boutonnieres are all alike.

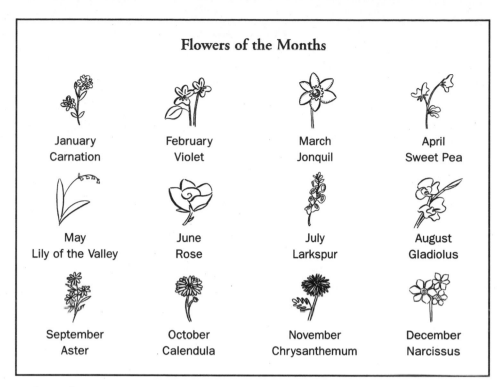

Flowers of the Months

January Carnation	February Violet	March Jonquil	April Sweet Pea
May Lily of the Valley	June Rose	July Larkspur	August Gladiolus
September Aster	October Calendula	November Chrysanthemum	December Narcissus

The Flower Girl

The flower girl walks ahead of the bride and carries a nosegay or a small basket decorated with flowers or ribbons. If the bride and groom wish, and the church or synagogue allows, the flower girl may scatter rose petals in the path of the bride. Because petals can be slippery, flower girls more often than not simply carry a basket or nosegay of flowers. A small headdress of flowers always looks adorable on a little girl.

Mothers and Grandmothers

The bride and groom may wish to provide corsages or single flowers for their mothers and grandmothers. Corsages and flowers not only honor those who wear them, they help guests identify special people with whom they may wish to exchange a few friendly words at the reception. Popular corsage flowers include gardenias, violets, daisies, and dainty cymbidium orchids, which come in all colors. Some women prefer not to wear corsages, so it is wise to check with mothers and grandmothers before ordering flowers. They may prefer to pin a single flower to a pocketbook.

Notes

Chapter Eleven

The Sound of Music

*Just as my fingers on these keys make music
So the selfsame sounds on my spirit make music too.*

WALLACE STEVENS

It is a gratifying experience to carefully select music that will make your wedding uniquely your own.

There are two distinct types of music that are usually played for most weddings. Inspiring, uplifting music is usually sung or played during the ceremony. Lively, entertaining music is usually played during the reception, especially when there is dancing. Sometimes two separate sets of musicians must be engaged. At other times, musicians are versatile enough to play music for both the ceremony and the reception. You also have the option of hiring an experienced wedding disc jockey to provide music for the ceremony and/or reception.

Music for the Ceremony

Weddings today employ a delightfully wide variety of musical genres and instruments. No longer is a soloist accompanied by an organ the only choice. Nowadays, any strings, woodwinds, brass, or vocals—or any combination thereof—may be used effectively.

Selecting Music

Yes, you will find that there are still some restrictions—particularly in houses of worship—and these vary from place to place. Eastern Orthodox churches, for instance, allow only vocal music, and Quakers allow no music whatsoever. It is important, therefore, that you discuss your proposed selections and instrumentation during your first visit to the clergymember's office. He or she may refer you to the organist, choir director, liturgist, or soloist for advice regarding selections that may and may not be played during the ceremony.

When selecting your music, you might go to a music shop and ask to hear a recording of wedding music, then make your own personal selections. Most music stores also carry songbooks containing music especially for weddings. Or an experienced wedding musician may be a source of song ideas.

Recordings of traditional wedding processionals and recessionals are available in the audio/visual sections of most libraries. Tapes and compact discs may also be ordered by calling Seven Veils Records at 800-388-2336.

Selecting Musicians

Your clergyperson should be able to recommend musicians. If your wedding will not take place at a house of worship, and you are not familiar with local musicians, check the yellow pages for listings of local music teachers' associations or the local musicians' union. Another good resource is the music department of a college or university. Music stores, too, usually keep lists of names they are happy to recommend.

When selecting a musician for your ceremony, it is wise to choose someone who will not panic—a professional or someone with a great deal of experience. Avoid accepting the offer of a friend or relative with little or no experience. A professional musician hired for a wedding is always paid, and time must be scheduled for him or her to practice with the accompanist or other musicians, if any. If a professional vocalist or musician is a relative or friend, the situation is a little tricky. You may offer payment, then let him or her decide whether to accept your offer. Often, a professional who charges a substantial fee for strangers will give music as a gift to friends or relatives. If a musician is a member of the wedding party, then a gift to him or her is appropriate.

Hiring Musicians

Musicians and disc jockeys usually set their fees according to their ability and experience. Remember to consider the amount of time the musicians spend both preparing and performing. If they must learn special music such as ethnic songs or circle dances, if they must practice with other instrumentalists, or if they will be present at the rehearsal, their fee is naturally more.

If the musicians hired for your ceremony will also be performing at your reception, they will expect to take a break during the reception and have something to eat and drink. This matter should be discussed early during negotiations.

Be sure to discuss what the musicians will be wearing. You do not want anyone showing up in blue jeans. Specify whether you expect the musicians to be dressed in formal attire.

After you've agreed on all details with musicians, sign a contract (this usually requires a down payment) and arrange for final payment in cash or by check when they are finished playing.

Music for a Ceremony in a House of Worship

The Prelude

The half-hour prior to the ceremony is the time to set the mood with music. Preludes may include favorite music (popular or classical) as well as vocal or instrumental solos. A solo is often sung just after the mother of the bride is seated.

Choose one or two of your favorite songs to set the mood. Combine these with traditional selections that include classical as well as popular tunes. I suggest "Theme from Romeo and Juliet" by Tchaikovsky, or the contemporary arrangements of Nino Rota. A vocal selection, such as "Sunrise, Sunset" from *Fiddler on the Roof,* may be sung while parents and grandparents are being seated.

The Processional

After the prelude, the processional begins. The processional music should be joyful, dignified, and majestic. It should have a regular beat so that the wedding party will feel comfortable walking slowly down the aisle in time with the music.

A traditional wedding march helps carry the spirits of all present along with the wedding party as they approach the altar. Two favorite pieces are "Wedding March" by Alexander Guilmant and "Marche Nuptiale" by Allan Caron.

Wagner's familiar bridal chorus from *Lohengrin* and Mendelssohn's "Wedding March" from *A Midsummer Night's Dream* were once considered inappropriate for Catholic weddings because of the pagan nature of the dramas. However, since the Second Vatican Council, restrictions have been lifted from these popular melodies, and they are now played regularly.

During the Ceremony

After the wedding party has reached the altar, special music usually announces the bride as she walks down the aisle. Sometimes music is played softly during the exchange of marriage vows, but this depends on the preferences of the bride and groom as well as the house of worship.

Musical selections played or sung during wedding ceremonies vary widely. Some churches allow classical or sacred music, while others are open to appropriate contemporary or secular pieces. Two classical pieces often used in weddings are "Ich Liebe Dich" by Grieg and "The Lord's Prayer" by Malotte. Popular contemporary songs include Peter, Paul, and Mary's "Wedding Song" ("There Is Love") and Andrew Lloyd Webber's "All I Ask of You" from *Phantom of the Opera*.

During the ceremony may be an appropriate time to dedicate a song to a loved one who has passed away or to introduce an ethnic song to cement a relationship with a family of foreign heritage.

The Recessional

At the end of the ceremony, the recessional begins triumphantly and has a slightly quicker tempo than the processional. The joyful spirit of the recessional music carries the wedding party up the aisle. Popular classical music selections are Mendelssohn's "Wedding March" from *A Midsummer Night's Dream* and "Trumpet Voluntary in D" by Purcell.

Music for a Second Wedding

Prelude music and music during the ceremony are of the same kind for a second wedding as for a first wedding. There are many sentimental vocal pieces that are favorites of all those caught up in the beauty and romance of love.

Q&A

Dear Edith,

We are getting married in a church and would like to select some good classical music. We would prefer not to have a soloist. Have you any suggestions?

ANSWER: The combination of a trumpet, oboe, and/or organ is very beautiful for a church wedding. Some pieces you may consider are Telemann's suite for trumpet or organ; Corelli's suite for oboe and organ; Baroque Composers' suite for trumpet and organ; Old German Lied for oboe and organ; or Handel's two arias for oboe, trumpet, and organ.

The main difference between music for first versus second weddings lies in the selection of processional and recessional music. For second weddings, many lean toward lighter nontraditional selections such as Purcell's "Westminster Abbey Hymn" or Bach's "Jesu, Joy of Man's Desiring" for the processional, and Handel's theme from *Water Music* for the recessional.

Music for a Ceremony in a Private Setting

There are, of course, no restrictions but your own good taste when it comes to choosing music for a ceremony in a home, club, or social hall. A pianist, harpist, or guitarist; a trio or quartet of any kind; or even compact discs are all acceptable options. Allow plenty of setup time for instruments. It is better to have the musicians waiting for you than for you to wait for them!

Recording the Ceremony Music on Tape

"I wish we had taped the music" is a sentiment often expressed by newlyweds after their wedding. Because of high emotions during the ceremony, the couple may not actually hear the sweet music played or remember the soft words spoken. Therefore, taping the ceremony for future enjoyment is worth considering. The tape may be especially welcomed by older family members and close friends who could not attend.

A sound recording of the ceremony may also be useful to a professional videographer. Some videocameras are unable to make high-quality sound recordings, so the videographer may choose to edit the videotape using the separate sound recording for background music. He or she may also create a videotape that plays the songs and words of the ceremony while showing still photographs. (See Chapter Twelve.)

Music for the Reception

Live Music

Light live music serves as a pleasant background while guests pass through the receiving line, socialize during the cocktail hour, and eat dinner. If there will be dancing later, music becomes the glue that holds the party together.

Decide what kind of mood you want to create, then find the right musicians to create it. Your personal music preference is your best choice, whether that be light classical music for easy listening, current popular songs, or dance music. Avoid playing alternative rock 'n' roll early in the evening, as this type of music may drive your older guests away fast! Give the musicians a good mix of songs to play and enough time to learn the music. Also, warn the band if Uncle Joe is apt to get up and play the saxophone during the reception. It will be much easier on the bandleader if he or she is forewarned.

If you cannot audition your musicians, most professionals can provide tapes for your review before you hire them. The musicians, for their part, will probably want to check the size and acoustics of the reception room so they will be able to select the right instruments and any necessary amplification.

If the musicians you hire belong to a union, their contract will require them to play for a specified time and then take a break. You might consider hiring another musician to play during breaks to keep spirits high.

Please do not assume that every musician knows what kind of music you need for each stage of your reception. I once attended a gorgeous wedding at which no one could socialize during dinner, because the music drowned out any hope of conversation. How disappointing it was for all the guests, who could not enjoy a warm reunion with friends and relatives they hadn't seen in years! A well-trained orchestra should be able to judge the right kind of music to play at the right time—but do not count on this. It is better to give specific instructions. Save the loud music for after-dinner dancing; it will be welcome then!

Any sentimental favorite songs that cannot be included in the wedding ceremony may be played during the reception. Some popular examples are Bette Midler's "The Wind beneath My Wings," Elton John's "Circle of Love," Lionel Richie's "Endless Love," Dan Fogelberg's "Longer," and Morris Albert's "Feelings." Other songs you might consider are "On a Wonderful Day Like Today," "Someone to Watch Over Me," and "The Girl That I Marry."

Disc Jockey

It is far more economical to hire a disc jockey to play compact discs than to hire live musicians. Some DJs will play only the music you request, and others will act as masters of ceremonies. In my opinion it is preferable to have the best man do the honors, but if he or another member of the wedding party is unable or unwilling to act as toastmaster, then a disc jockey may.

A skilled DJ should be familiar with wedding protocol. He or she should introduce members of the wedding party; signal when it is time for the bride and groom to dance the first dance; and announce the cutting of the wedding cake, the throwing of the bridal bouquet, and any other customs you wish to observe at your reception. One must select a DJ with great care—check references and ask who will be his or her backup in case of illness. You do not want to end up with an inexperienced, insensitive, or overbearing disc jockey who spoils your wedding.

Electrical Wiring at a Home Reception

If you will be holding a reception at home, it is very important to check the house's wiring system to be sure it can handle all the equipment used by cooks, musicians, and lighting engineers. It may be wise to talk to a professional electrician. He or she can tell you what power is available in the house, what various equipment will require, and whether you will need to rent a portable generator.

Notes

Chapter Twelve

Photographs and Videotapes

Above all, I craved to seize the whole essence, in the confines of one single photograph of some situation that was in the process of unrolling itself before my eyes.

HENRI CARTIER-BRESSON

Photographs

Choosing a Photographer

The best way to choose a photographer is to visit his or her studio, carefully review sample albums, and openly discuss your photographic budget.

I strongly recommend choosing an experienced professional wedding photographer over a portrait photographer. An experienced wedding photographer has been trained to follow many social conventions; this will help you avoid unnecessary irritations. You do not want him or her showing up in a T-shirt and jeans or barging into the refreshment line ahead of your guests—but these things can and do happen! Similarly, overbearing and rude photographers have upset many a bride and groom.

Wedding photos are important—there will be no second chance to get them right—and a photographer who specializes in weddings can be a joy not only on your wedding day but also for a lifetime, as you treasure his or her work. Long after the flowers have wilted, the cake has been eaten, the guests have returned home, and the gifts have worn out, the photographs will remain to bring alive your memorable wedding day!

Be sure to interview prospective photographers before hiring one. During the interview, find out what services the photographer will provide at what price. Most wedding photographers offer several different packages. Do you want black-and-white or color photos? How many shots will be taken? How much time will the photographer spend? Will the photographer provide negatives only? Does the service include proofs, prints, and/or an album?

Most photographers ask for a deposit when they take on an assignment and expect full payment upon delivery of the photographs. How much of a deposit is required? How much will it cost you or the members of the wedding party to have duplicate prints made up? There should be a reduction in price for ordering photos in quantity.

Most importantly, you should find out who the actual photographer will be. Will it be the owner of the studio or an assistant? Confirm all arrangements in writing. And remember that photographing a wedding from beginning to end can take as long as eight hours. A wedding photographer deserves to be offered a meal.

The bride and groom usually present a formal wedding photograph or an enlarged candid to their parents. Wedding photos also make thoughtful thank-you gifts for attendants. The bride and groom may wish to furnish appropriate photos to friends or relatives as well. If anyone desires additional photos, refer him or her to the photographer, for it is best for individuals to purchase photos directly.

Possible Photographs

- The bride and groom may pose for a formal engagement portrait.
- The bride and groom may have a formal studio wedding portrait taken before the wedding for newspaper release. Studio photos are superior to candids taken on the wedding day.
- The photographer may take candid photos at home before the wedding.
- The photographer may shoot photos at the church and/or during the ceremony.
- Photos taken at the reception may be formal pictures of the bride and groom alone, with the bridesmaids, with the groomsmen, and with the entire wedding party. Photos of the couple with each set of parents and other members of the immediate family follow these. In case of divorced parents, each parent usually has a separate photo taken with the couple. Stepparents are included if they are on close terms with the bride and groom.
- Candid photos may also be taken at the reception. These might include photos of guests, the bride and groom cutting the cake, and the bride throwing her bouquet. For candid photographs at the reception, it is wise to provide the photographer with a list of special people you wish to have photographed. You might say, "Please be sure to take a picture of my

Dear Edith,

How can we cut down on long photograph sessions after the ceremony or during the reception? We would like to socialize with our guests as much as possible.

ANSWER: There are several ways this goal may be achieved. Most photographers who specialize in weddings recommend taking as many pictures as possible of the bride, groom, and wedding party before the wedding ceremony. The professional photographer then needs only to take candid shots during the reception, along with some posed shots of the cake cutting, bouquet throwing, dancing, and so on.

Another approach that works well under some circumstances is to hire the professional photographer to take family group photos before the rehearsal or rehearsal dinner. This cuts down considerably on photographing at the reception.

It is helpful to make in advance a list of group photographs you would like to have taken. Allow sufficient time to assemble the group. Remember, people scatter at a reception, and it takes a lot more time to gather a group together. Some photos may be easier to take at the rehearsal dinner or before the ceremony.

grandparents with my parents." Then designate someone to point these people out to the photographer.

Photos before the Ceremony

In order to avoid keeping guests waiting between the ceremony and reception, many couples have their formal wedding photos taken before the ceremony.

Photos in Church

Some churches have restrictions regarding photographs taken during the wedding ceremony. Sometimes flash photography is prohibited. A skilled photographer should be able to take beautiful photos without using a flash. The photographer should be as inconspicuous as possible throughout the ceremony. Ushers should ask wedding guests who arrive with cameras to refrain from taking flash pictures in the sanctuary, as this may seriously interfere with the work of the professional photographer. It also greatly detracts from the solemnity of the occasion to have clicking and flashing lights go off during the ceremony. Alternatively, a memo regarding flash photography may be added to the wedding program.

Photos at the Reception

Instead of keeping guests waiting endlessly between the ceremony and the reception while the wedding party has formal pictures taken, many couples prefer to take family pictures after all the guests have passed through the receiving line at the reception. Guests should avoid taking flash photos until after the professional photographer has finished working. When posing for pictures, be sure to give some thought to the background, as many good shots have been spoiled when taken in front of an open kitchen door or a view of the parking lot.

Disposable Cameras

Disposable cameras have become very popular at weddings. These may be placed on tables for guests to use freely. A basket may be provided for deposit of the cameras after the reception.

Amateur Photographers

A friend may offer to take your wedding photos, but do not trust your once-in-a-lifetime memories to a once-in-a-while photographer! This may be risky for a good many reasons, so it is best to decline the offer graciously. As a guest at your wedding, your friend may be off somewhere having a good time (and isn't that why he or she was invited?) just when you are cutting the cake or throwing the bouquet. There is also the possibility that your friend is not as skilled a photographer as he or she wishes to be. To avoid hurt feelings, suggest that your friend take some extra candids before the wedding or at the reception, and encourage him or her to have a good time and not worry about having to take photos.

Videotapes

To Tape or Not to Tape

Today's bride, groom, and clergyperson must decide how to handle the delicate matter of videotaping a wedding. Some people have already come to positive conclusions and are enthusiastic about documenting their wedding in this way. Some people are on the fence about it, and others have not even considered doing it.

If you have never considered videotaping your wedding or have even been opposed to the idea, you may be interested in the words of one couple: "What a switch from our determination not to tape! Now we feel that the videotape is the most important plan we made. It brings back so many wonderful memories."

There are two good reasons you may wish to have your wedding videotaped: (1) It will be a pleasure to replay the tape in years to come; and (2) it is thoughtful to show a videotape of the wedding to a special member of the family who was unable to attend.

Before hiring a videographer, be sure to review a sample of his or her work. You may find that what some professionals have in mind is not at all what you expect!

What to Tape

Decide if you would like to begin videotaping before, during, or after the ceremony. Perhaps you would like to start with scenes shot at a shower, the rehearsal dinner, or just before the ceremony at the bride and/or groom's home. (Some couples may not object to a few candid shots as they put on finishing touches, while others might prefer complete privacy.) Or perhaps you would rather begin your videotape with scenes of the wedding party leaving home for the ceremony or arriving at the ceremony site. Perhaps you would prefer to videotape only at the reception.

How the ceremony is videotaped depends on the wishes of the officiant and the skill of the videographer. Some clergymembers will not give permission to videotape at all. Others will insist that the videographer work from only one location, such as a balcony. Still others will permit a skilled videographer to move about quietly and unobtrusively using available light. The videographer should attend the rehearsal to familiarize him- or herself with possible camera positions, lighting problems, and the timing of the ceremony. If a professional photographer will also be on the scene, communication and cooperation between the two is essential. Each professional should be alerted in advance about the other.

Videotaping the wedding party as they leave the ceremony site and arrive at the reception should create no problem for anyone. Scenes of the receiving line, the feasting, toasting, dancing, cake cutting, garter doffing, bouquet throwing, and so on can be sources of immeasurable pleasure for the whole family.

Editing

There are two kinds of editing that can be done on videotape. You might choose to have the videographer edit while shooting. This method takes more advance planning, but it requires no cutting, is far less expensive, and allows you to see your videotape right away. The other option is professional editing after the wedding, which can take up to twenty hours of a videographer's time, may be quite costly, and requires you to wait before you can view the finished product.

Whichever method you choose, skillful planning and editing can provide special touches to enhance your videotape. A close-up photo of the wedding invitation might introduce the program. The videotape might show the exterior of the bride and/or groom's house and the ceremony site with the site's name visible. It might also show stained-glass windows, exterior and interior scenes of the reception site, a close-up of the buffet table before the guests arrive, a close-up of the flower arrangements, a shot of the musicians, a close-up of the wedding cake, and so on.

You may wish to record the music played during your ceremony, and run this in the background throughout your videotape. Speaking of sound, I was particularly charmed when, while viewing one of my family wedding tapes, I heard the sound of birds chirping merrily as everyone waited to enter the church.

Budget

If you are eager to have a high-quality videotape of your wedding, and your budget allows, it is best to hire an experienced wedding videographer. Give him or her a script of the wedding day, a roster of special people to be videotaped, and a wish list of stills and action shots. A family member may be assigned to assist in identifying people.

If you are on a limited budget, you may choose to rent a videocamera for a day and have someone reliable operate it for you, or you may accept the kind offer of a friend or relative who owns a videocamera. The results range from mediocre to terrific—but nothing ventured, nothing gained.

Videotaping Still Photographs

Some professional wedding photographers now offer an attractive service that is well worth considering. Still photographs of your wedding may be transferred onto videotape and accompanied by a soundtrack that includes readings, vows, ceremony music, toasts, and reception music. You may even add custom captions and graphics, if you wish.

If a professionally edited videotape is out of the question, and you don't wish to have a videographer edit while shooting or risk assigning an amateur videographer, a video wedding album may be just the thing for you. The still photos fade in and out gracefully and sequentially, creating a very professional-looking photographic memory. You may choose either a short version to be shown to friends or a longer version to be shown to family.

Additional ideas for a video wedding album include photographs from the lives of the bride and groom, beginning with childhood and following through their first meeting and engagement. This stroll down memory lane may be shown to the guests at the reception.

There is no limit on what may be added at a future date! Photos of the honeymoon, anniversaries, birthdays, pictures of the children, holidays, and so on are all good possibilities. The bride and groom may build a library of important memories and milestones on videotape for everlasting enjoyment.

Newspaper Photographs

Check with the society editor of your local newspaper regarding photographic requirements. Generally, newspapers ask for an eight-by-ten-inch black-and-white glossy print. Most papers have a form to be filled out so an article can be written to accompany your photo.

Makeup

One way the female members of the wedding party can help the photographer take beautiful photos is by applying makeup properly. No makeup at all may make photos appear washed out and anemic. Too much makeup will look theatrical, and heavy false eyelashes will cast unwanted shadows. Ideally, makeup should look natural. Some brides engage a professional makeup artist to serve any attendants who wish to participate.

Following are some helpful hints from international makeup expert Glenna Franklin:

1. It is not necessary to buy expensive products. Most department stores and drugstores carry adequate supplies, and your own favorite makeup may be used.

2. Choose foundation in a shade close to your skin tone. If the foundation is too dark, it will create a masklike effect.

3. Apply concealer with a sponge to cover undereye circles or blemishes. Next, apply foundation smoothly into the hairline. Cover face and neck with a fine powder and blend well with a brush. Avoid shiny skin because camera flashes may produce a glare that is almost impossible to remove from photos.

4. Use soft brown pencil for eyeliner. Apply brown powder using a sponge-tipped applicator on top of eyeliner to set it and prevent smearing.

5. Use black or brown mascara. Do not use pale or frosted eye makeup.

6. Keep the shape of your eyebrows natural and color brows lightly with a soft, gentle stroke.

7. Apply a touch of rouge or blush high on your cheekbones and blend carefully.

8. Use a lipliner pencil and outline your natural lip line. (This helps prevent lipstick from running.) Blend with a cotton swab and cover with pastel lipstick. Add a touch of gloss in center of lower lip.

Eyeglasses

Even if you always wear eyeglasses and feel they are a part of you, consider taking them off for formal photographs. Glasses can produce glare that detracts from a photograph. Also, styles in eyeglasses change, so eyeglasses may quickly date a photo. Finally, eyeglasses hide facial features and family resemblances in brows, noses, and eyes. If you will be posing for any studio portraits and wish to wear eyeglasses, you may be able to remove your lenses and wear the frames only.

Notes

Chapter Thirteen

Gifts

The great secret of successful marriage is to treat all disasters as incidents and none of the incidents as disasters.

HAROLD NICHOLSON

Gift Registry

There are no disadvantages—only advantages—when you decide to register for wedding gifts in a department, jewelry, or gift store. Gift registry is a free service that appeals to the bride and groom, the shopper, and the store itself for the following good reasons:

- A bride and groom who register for gifts can share in the fun of choosing items they will be delighted to receive. They also help guests by providing ideas for gifts that will be cherished for years to come. The couple may choose colors and designs to fit their home décor; they may select dishware, glassware, and flatware that harmonize with each other; and they can cut down enormously on the time it might take to return or exchange three toasters, six hideous orange bath towels, and a queen-sized blanket for a king-sized bed.
- A shopper who uses a gift registry can avoid all uncertainty. He or she can quickly and easily choose a gift that is sure to be well received and that is within his or her budget.
- A store that offers gift registry cuts down on costly returns and time-consuming exchanges. Gift registry also attracts additional business.

The Consultant

Because gift registry brings in many customers who may need assistance in making decisions, a store with a registry usually has a consultant on staff. The consultant fills out a form for each couple and records their choices for tableware, linens, kitchen accessories, and so on. Some stores computerize this information and share it with affiliated stores. When registering, be sure to ask the consultant which stores have access to your list and whether it will be sent automatically or if it must be requested.

Registering for wedding gifts can be a pleasure when you make an appointment with an experienced consultant in a fine shop or in a department store's main branch, which will carry a wide selection of housewares. Registering can be a big headache if you drop in at a branch store where a part-time, so-called consultant without any training or experience is on duty. Shop around until you find the right person to advise you. Good consultants are out there!

This is the sage advice you'll hear from an experienced consultant: "Take your time in making your selections. Come back and look around again (and again, if necessary). Housewares cost a lot of money, and you'll have to live with your choices for a long time. Don't choose hastily."

Some consultants are extremely knowledgeable and can point out, for example, the different characteristics of bone china, stoneware, ironware, and earthenware. They know which designs are open stock and which are likely to be discontinued. They can explain the advantages and disadvantages of new materials. Even couples who know what they like should listen to what the consultant has to say.

Choosing Patterns and Styles

Usually a couple choose their dishware pattern first and build around that. Consultants have long been encouraging couples to select all-white dishware. Yes, white is dramatic in its simplicity and goes with everything, but a pattern can be equally dramatic (and original) if a whole room's décor is built around a spectacular design. In addition, a china pattern with an attractive, colorful border provides an automatic "garnish" for food, which makes every meal look appetizing. Stop and think about this for a moment: Many delicious foods (mashed potatoes, cauliflower, noodles, rice, chicken, fish, and meat) lack eye appeal because they lack color. To make an attractive presentation, you need to add colorful vegetables and garnishes, particularly when using an all-white plate.

A bride and groom who register for wedding gifts must remember that registering does not ensure receipt of a complete set of anything. Wedding gifts are meant to give newlyweds a start in their homemaking, and family members are usually delighted to add to the collection on birthdays and anniversaries.

Admittedly, being confronted with hundreds of styles of different housewares can be very confusing. My advice to every couple is to think about the way you like to dress. Most people know if they are the tailored, traditional type or the casual, comfortable type; the sporty or sophisticated type; the crafty or ethnic type; or the muted or bold type. Once you pinpoint your clothing style, you can translate that into home-décor selections that reflect the real you.

Before registering, it is a good idea to think about your probable future lifestyle. Do you both come from large families, which may mean a lot of entertaining? If so, then concentrate on a complete set of tableware. Do you adore cooking? If so, register for a slew of timesaving kitchen appliances. Do your jobs demand a lot of travel? Then you may prefer choosing sturdy lifetime luggage. Do you expect to inherit some treasured heirlooms? Then choose designs that will be compatible.

When registering, select a wide price range from which friends and relatives can choose. It is possible that two or three friends may wish to purchase one important piece together. Or someone may be looking for a simple shower gift or may want to buy two small items instead of one large one.

By the way, it is perfectly acceptable to register at more than one store. You may, for example, want to register for linens at one store and for tableware at another store.

When family and friends are scattered all over the country, it is advantageous to register at a national department store, but remember that selections registered at a store in San Francisco may not automatically go to all stores nationwide. A smart couple will register not only in their hometown, but also in the town where most family and friends live. If you've registered at a store that promises automatic sharing of registry information, it pays to call and check that the service is working.

The Second Time Around

Should people getting married a second time register for wedding gifts? Of course they should! This service can be a real blessing to friends and relatives. It is also helpful for couples who will be attempting to mesh a hodgepodge of housewares from their individual lives.

Registering for wedding gifts helps fill gaps that gradually appear over the years—even in the most complete household. Are your old mono-grammed towels getting frayed? Do you have a motley collection of nine red wine glasses, four white wine glasses, and three on-the-rocks glasses? Do you need an up-to-date kitchen accessory? Might a small tree or flower-ing shrub complete your landscaping? Would a painting or an antique fill an empty wall? What about a contribution to a favorite charity? A well-selected gift means just as much to someone marrying for the second time as it does to someone who has never been married before.

Money! Money! Money!

It is tempting for some couples to ask for money instead of gifts, and many have inquired about how this can be done gracefully. The answer is: It cannot. There is no way to *ask* for money gracefully. If family members are asked what the couple might like, they may suggest giving cash, but remember that most people prefer to give gifts by which they will be remembered as time goes by.

Registering at a Travel Agency

Some established, reliable travel agencies that are members of the American Society of Travel Agents (headquartered in Washington, D.C.) will register couples for honeymoons. They may offer special cruises, ski trips, or other packages that appeal to you. What happens if the registry does not cover the cost of the honeymoon? The newlyweds likely will have to pay the difference, or they may have to cut back on luxuries. Travel agents will request payment in full before the trip is ticketed.

Sharing the Pleasure

A good way to build bridges between two families is for the bride to inform the groom's parents of gifts that have been sent by their friends, and for the groom to do the same for the bride's parents. A simple list may be telephoned or mailed from time to time, both before and after the wed-ding. Then, when the parents see their friends, they will have the pleasure of thanking the friends sincerely and telling them that their gift has been received and is admired.

Displaying Gifts

Some families follow the charming custom of displaying wedding gifts. Sometimes a special day is set aside for friends and relatives to visit the bride's home and share a few light refreshments. If the wedding reception is at the home of parents, gifts may be attractively displayed there on a long, draped table for guests to admire. (Checks are not displayed in any setting.)

Displaying permits close relatives and friends to ooh and ah over all the gifts at one time. However, it does take a good deal of time and space—not to mention a tremendous amount of skill and tact—to arrange all the gifts tastefully and in such a way that people won't notice duplications. It also means the gifts can't be exchanged until after the honeymoon.

Instead of displaying gifts before the wedding, it may be more convenient to invite friends to the newlyweds' home after the wedding, where they will have the pleasure of seeing their gifts in their proper settings.

There is no fixed rule for displaying gifts—it is mostly a matter of space, convenience, and local custom.

Dear Edith,
We're invited to attend a wedding, but we cannot go to the reception. Should we bring our wedding gift to the church?

ANSWER: Chances are, there will be no one to receive your gift at the church. It is much better to have the gift delivered to the bride or groom's home before the wedding.

Insuring Gifts

Gifts may be insured by a floating policy, which usually lasts three months and also may cover damage incurred during shipping. If a wedding has been highly publicized, it is wise to hire a guard when away from home or during the rehearsal, ceremony, and reception.

Broken Gifts

When a gift arrives broken, the first thing to do is to determine if the package was sent from a store, in which case the gift is probably insured and will be replaced by the store. If the gift was sent by the giver via a shipping company (such as UPS), the gift must remain in its original carton for inspection, and a claim must be filed immediately with the company. If the gift was mailed through United States Mail and was insured, you must take it to a post office in its original package to file a claim.

If a gift arrives broken but is not insured, you might consider writing a thank-you note without mentioning the mishap.

Missing Gift Cards

Occasionally, a store will slip up and omit a gift card. If this happens, notify the store, and it will trace the sale and inform you of the giver.

Monogramming and Engraving

When Anne Lovejoy marries Robert Baldwin, the traditional linen monogram (assuming that both take the surname Baldwin) would be a large *B* in the center flanked by two smaller letters. The bride's first-name initial, *A,* would go on the left, and her maiden-surname initial, *L,* would go on the right:

$$A\,B\,L$$

If the letters were to be all the same size, the monogram would read:

$$A\,B\,L$$

If one initial were to be used, it would be *B*.

There are many ways to engrave silver, and most jewelers will be able to help you decide how to engrave yours. When a single letter is used, it may be the first letter of the bride and/or groom's surname. When three letters are used, they may be arranged in the same way as the traditional linen monogram. Alternatively, three letters may be arranged with a large surname initial centered above or below two smaller letters (the bride or groom's first-name initials). Using this method, Anne Lovejoy and Robert Baldwin's silver monogram might read:

$$\mathcal{AL}$$
$$\mathcal{B}$$

Gifts for the Wedding Party

We are all familiar with the saying "It is better to give than to receive." Unfortunately, we are not often told what to give.

It is customary for the bride and groom to give each of their attendants a thank-you gift for helping make their wedding memorable. Naturally, the gift should reflect the taste and budget of the couple. It need not be expensive, but it should be something that will have lasting meaning.

The bride may select a special gift (different from the gifts to her bridesmaids, which are usually identical) for her maid or matron of honor, junior bridesmaid, or flower girl. The groom may do the same for his best man or ring bearer.

The bride may present her gifts at a bridesmaids' luncheon, and the groom may present his gifts at a bachelor party. Alternatively, the couple could present all their gifts at the rehearsal dinner.

For the Bride's Attendants

An appropriate gift for a bridesmaid or flower girl might be a piece of jewelry (pin, bracelet, necklace, or earrings—real or costume) to be worn at the wedding. The jewelry might be monogrammed or dated. Another option is to give each attendant a small monogrammed and dated silver or gold frame. Such frames are usually available in jewelry stores. Yet another option is a china or glass mug or plate monogrammed and dated by an artist. Such gifts are usually available in fine gift shops. If the bride herself is artistic, she may choose to create a memento that reflects her skill in sewing, weaving, painting, calligraphy, embroidery, or needlepoint.

For the Groom's Attendants

Jewelry stores carry a wide selection of men's gifts that may be engraved with initials and a date. These include: small picture frames, silver boxes, small clocks, letter or bottle openers, money clips, key rings, cuff links, belt buckles, tie bars, mugs, or luggage tags. The groom might also choose gifts pertaining to his attendants' favorite hobbies, sports, music, or books. Such gifts can be found in specialty catalogues as well as at shopping malls.

Exchange of Gifts by the Bride and Groom

Some brides and grooms exchange wedding gifts with each other, and this exchange may take place at any suitable time. A gift of jewelry, a family heirloom, a rare book, or any token of one's affection may be given before or after the ceremony or during the honeymoon.

Gifts for Children from a Previous Marriage

Many brides and grooms who are parents of young children from a previous marriage wish to involve the children in their wedding ceremony and recognize the newly established family with a memento of the occasion. This may be done with the blessing of the officiant, who may include the youngster(s) during the exchange of rings. The officiant may present a boy with a medallion or ring set with his birthstone and engraved with the bride and groom's names or initials and the wedding date. The officiant may present a girl with a small engraved locket, bracelet, or ring set with her birthstone.

Favors

The origin of favors goes back to earlier times, when touching a bride and groom was considered lucky! Guests would snatch flowers from the bride's bouquet or help themselves to a souvenir by tearing off ribbons or bits of lace from the bride's dress.

Today it is customary for the bride and groom to give each guest a memento of their wedding for good luck. Favors may be candied almonds wrapped in tulle, small candy boxes containing two truffles each, mints personalized with the couple's initials, or small, custom-labeled bottles of wine. For the environmentally conscious, seed packets, miniature herb wreaths, or tiny saplings are welcome gifts.

Just about anything with a wedding theme may make suitable favors, including candles, tiny picture frames, and monogrammed golf balls. However, you might remember the advice given recently by the prominent special-events planner Colin Cowie: "Don't spend money on favors; put it in the food!"

Notes

Chapter Fourteen

Transportation

*What is not good for the hive
is not good for the bee.*

MARCUS AURELIUS

When someone asks what he or she can do to help with your wedding, the perfect assignment (if this person likes to organize and direct) is the arrangement of reliable transportation. This includes transportation from home to ceremony and from ceremony to reception for all members of the wedding party. There must be plenty of cars that are clean inside and out and that have full gas tanks.

Naturally, you must know the number of people who require transportation in order to estimate the number of cars needed. The availability of parking must also be carefully evaluated at all three locations (home, ceremony site, and reception site). If a traffic problem is likely, you may wish to notify the police in advance so an officer can supervise parking or handle any bottlenecks on the wedding day.

Maps

It is wise to provide maps for out-of-town guests and volunteer drivers. Maps should be clearly marked with place names, addresses, street names, and directions. They may be drawn by hand or computer and photocopied. They may also be printed on the back of the wedding programs.

Author Robert Louis Stevenson once sent a note to his friend James Barrie inviting Mr. Barrie to visit him on the island of Samoa in the South Pacific. The note read: "You take the boat at San Francisco, then my place is the second on the left." The world's geography has become a bit more complex since this simple note was written, so a detailed map with explicit directions is advisable for your wedding. It will keep your guests from getting confused, frustrated, lost, and delayed.

Special Transportation Cards

A variety of cards may be enclosed with the wedding invitation or given to out-of-town guests when they arrive. For example, a travel card might explain that you have chartered a bus or ferry for transporting guests to an out-of-the-way site: "Shepler's Ferry will transport you to the island and back. Please present this card at the ticket office." Or a parking card might explain that you have arranged free parking for guests: "Parking is provided at the adjacent garage on Front Street. Gratuities are included. Please present this card to the attendant."

Who Leaves Home First?

At a traditional formal wedding, the bride's mother and several bridesmaids leave first in one car, and they are followed by the rest of the attendants in as many cars as are necessary. The last car transports the bride and her father to the ceremony.

After the ceremony, the bride and groom are the first to leave for the reception. They are followed by both sets of parents, then the attendants.

Transportation Choices

To add spice to their trip from ceremony to reception, the bride and groom may consider riding in an open convertible, an antique car, or a horse-drawn carriage or sleigh. Their choice will, of course, depend on the locale and time of year.

For a formal wedding, a limousine is another desirable option. Limousines are spacious, elegant, and clean, and it is relaxing to sit back and be transported by a competent, uniformed professional driver. In urban communities, consult the yellow pages to find limousine rental companies.

Use the same caution when selecting a limousine service as you would when doing business with any unfamiliar company. The National Limousine Association requires its members to have proper licensing and insurance. Ask each company if it offers any special wedding packages. Ask if the driver and backup driver are familiar with the area. Be sure to get your agreement in writing. Ask about any required deposit or extra fees and gratuities. Be sure to make arrangements if the driver will have to wait.

Friends May Help

Friends may offer to drive out-of-town guests, elderly relatives, or members of the wedding party to the ceremony and reception. In return, you may offer them a gift certificate for gasoline and a car wash or any other suitable present.

Valet Parking

When the wedding is large and parking is at a premium, it is thoughtful to provide valet parking. In a small community, it may be possible to engage high-school students or athletic team members who will channel their profits toward a school project. In a large city, professional parking services are widely available.

Dear Edith,
We were very pleased with the driver of the limousine for our daughter's wedding. He was most helpful in a crunch. Is it proper to give him a tip, or would this be resented?

ANSWER: As a general rule, a tip is only refused when it is a matter of company policy. Even if a tip is refused, rest assured that the offer is never resented.

Many wonder when to tip in cash and when to tip with a gift. You should never tip professionals such as doctors, lawyers, and accountants with money, but it is perfectly acceptable to show your appreciation with a gift. And you are always free to give a gift instead of cash to anyone who provides a special service, whether it is your driver, hairdresser, chef, or florist.

If someone has helped you when you ran out of gas, had a flat tire, or confronted a crisis and has refused to accept a tip, he or she may accept it if you say: "Please give this to your favorite charity or to your church."

Decorating the Newlyweds' Car

It is usually up to the groomsmen to decorate the newlyweds' getaway car with flower garlands, streamers, balloons, and/or signs sometime during the reception. The windshield should be left clear so as not to obstruct the driver's vision. The car decorators should also make sure they decorate the right car. If the car is borrowed or rented, the decorations should be kept to a minimum and should avoid using glue, tape, rubber cement, paint, or any other chemicals that may damage the car's finish.

Notes

Notes

Chapter Fifteen

The Rehearsal and Ceremony

To be prepared is half the victory.

CERVANTES

The Rehearsal

The best insurance for a perfect ceremony—whether you are having an informal home wedding with twenty-five guests or a cathedral wedding with hundreds—is a rehearsal.

Without a rehearsal, people tend to bump into each other, turn the wrong way, enter and exit awkwardly, do things at the wrong time or forget to do them at all, and be generally nervous and uneasy. The beauty of a wedding is greatly enhanced when all these little problems are worked out ahead of time.

Those who should attend the rehearsal are the officiant (or a stand-in), the bride and groom, their parents, all the attendants, the musician(s), anyone who will participate in the cermony (such as a reader), and possibly the photographer and/or videographer.

If the wedding ceremony will take place in a house of worship, the clergymember may choose to speak during the rehearsal about the religious meaning of the ceremony. This helps put everyone at ease and fosters understanding about the event that is about to occur.

The rehearsal should be held at the ceremony site in order to practice the processional, the recessional, and any other parts of the ceremony during which timing is critical. Everyone needs to know how long it will take to get from one place to another, and the musicians need cues.

Before the Rehearsal

As soon as the wedding party is assembled at the ceremony site, all should be shown exactly where they will be standing during the ceremony.

Dear Edith,

We are having our wedding rehearsal on a Friday, the day before our wedding. People are coming from all over, and no one knows anyone. What can we do to liven things up and help the attendants get to know each other?

ANSWER: T-shirts may be your answer! On the front of each T-shirt, print "I survived the (bride's name) and (groom's name) wedding (date)." The back of each shirt can identify the wearer: "bride," "groom," "best man," "mother of the bride," and so forth. You might also have caps printed for the entire wedding party, use poster board and marker to make signs to be hung around the neck, or create simple paper headbands. Any gimmick that helps people loosen up and get acquainted will do!

After everyone knows exactly where he or she will be standing, then the wedding party can begin practicing how to get there.

Aisles

If the ceremony takes place in a house of worship that has two main aisles and no center aisle, one aisle may be ignored. You can block off one section so that guests are seated only in the sections that flank the aisle being used. This technique works well if the house of worship will not be full. Alternatively, the wedding party may process down one aisle at the beginning of the ceremony and recess up the other aisle at the end. This technique works well if the house of worship will be full.

If only one aisle is used, the bride's parents are seated on one side of the aisle and the groom's parents on the other side. If both aisles are used, both sets of parents are seated in the center front row.

Directing the Rehearsal

The rehearsal will proceed smoothly and efficiently if one knowledgeable person is in charge. If no one directs the rehearsal, there may be long, unnecessary discussions and disagreements.

Some clergymembers prefer to be in complete charge of rehearsals for weddings that will be held in their places of worship. A clergyperson is very familiar with his or her worship space and may have decided preferences as to how things are done. If he or she is not interested in all the details of a wedding, an associate or a wedding coordinator may direct the rehearsal.

Children in the Wedding Party

It is not necessary for small children in the wedding party to stand during the entire ceremony or to take part in the recessional. During the rehearsal, they may be instructed to be seated with their parents at a designated time.

After the Rehearsal

After the ceremony rehearsal, ushers should practice escorting people to their seats, remembering any special seating arrangements. For a wedding in a house of worship, ushers should also practice dismissing the guests pew by pew.

Before adjourning the rehearsal, the wedding party should gather to go over any unanswered questions.

If the officiant permits, the bride, groom, and witnesses (usually the best man and maid or matron of honor) may now sign the wedding license and certificate of marriage.

When the rehearsal is over, the entire wedding party may relax and look forward with pleasure to the rehearsal dinner.

The Christian Wedding

The Processional

In the traditional Christian wedding, the officiant faces the bride and groom, and the attendants stand on both sides of the couple. The bride and her attendants stand on the left, and the groom and his attendants stand on the right. (This arrangement usually applies to guests, too—the bride's family and friends are seated on the left, and the groom's family and friends are seated on the right.)

Traditionally, the groom and best man enter from the side at the officiant's signal and wait at the altar. The groomsmen process down the aisle first in pairs, the shorter ones preceding the taller ones. Next come the bridesmaids in pairs and by height. The maid or matron of honor follows alone. If there is a ring bearer, he comes next. The flower girl, if any, precedes the bride. The bride walks down the aisle on the arm of her father or a male relative. (He should walk on the side where he will be sitting so that he does not have to step over the bride's train to be seated.) If there are any pages, they follow the bride and carry her train.

Other options include having the groomsmen escort the bridesmaids down the aisle or having the bride enter alone, escorted by her mother, or escorted by both parents.

Many guests feel that the processional is one of the most enjoyable parts of the entire wedding day. They enjoy observing the wedding party moving slowly down the aisle. They admire the attractive attendants, the radiant bride in her beautiful gown, and the lush flowers, and they enjoy listening to the bride and groom's favorite music. The pomp and elegance of the processional provides a touching memory for everyone.

To make the most of this precious moment, it is essential that all members of the wedding party walk very slowly. They should start down the aisle left foot first and stay four pews apart. (This usually takes a bit of practice, as many young people are anxious to tear down the aisle.) They should walk erectly but not stiffly. They should try to look straight ahead, but if they happen to catch someone's eye, they may give a little smile of recognition.

The bride should count eight beats of music (or allow double the space between the attendants) before she proceeds down the aisle. The wedding party should face the bride as she walks down the aisle. The music should stop when the bride reaches the chancel steps.

The Ceremony

When the ceremony begins, the attendants turn to face the altar. They should not stand shoulder to shoulder, forming a wall in front of the seated guests. It is much more graceful if they stand at a three-quarter turn. This helps focus attention on the bride and groom, provides a feeling of openness, and allows guests a better view of the altar area.

In a traditional ceremony, the officiant may ask, "Who gives this woman in holy matrimony?" The bride's father and/or mother or a close relative may respond with "I do," "Her mother/father and I do," or "We do." If a parent is too ill or infirm to walk down the aisle, he or she may be seated in a pew or a wheelchair just before the processional and may respond to the question from there.

Many women today consider the idea of giving the bride away archaic and choose to omit the custom described above. An alternative is a pledge by both sets of parents to lovingly support the couple in their marriage relationship.

During the rest of the ceremony rehearsal, the clergymember usually instructs the wedding party regarding the sequence of events, and the bride and groom practice their vows, the blessing and exchange of rings, and any kneeling, rising, or other movements (such as the lighting of a unity candle) that will take place.

The Unity Candle

The lighting of a unity candle is a fairly recent custom compared to the age-old exchange of rings. Some couples choose to observe this custom to emphasize their unity and symbolize the blending of their two families. Each set of parents lights one of two small candles that flank a larger candle, and these remain burning throughout the ceremony. The large candle remains unlit until after the officiant pronounces the couple husband and wife. At this time, the bride and groom use the two small candles to light the unity candle together. (Some couples light their unity candles again on each wedding anniversary to renew their commitment.)

If divorced parents are on friendly terms, they may be glad to perform their role in the unity candle ceremony together. Otherwise, it is best to discuss the lighting of the unity candle with the officiant or omit the ceremony altogether.

The End of the Ceremony

At the end of the traditional Christian ceremony, the groom has the honor of being the first man to kiss his new wife. At a large formal church wedding, the kiss is frequently omitted. At this point, the officiant may introduce the newlyweds to the guests as "Mr. and Mrs."

For an informal garden wedding, the officiant may elect to introduce the newlyweds and have the couple remain where they are standing to receive the guests, omitting a recessional.

The Recessional

After a traditional church ceremony, the bride and groom lead the recessional, followed by the maid or matron of honor. The groomsmen may escort the bridesmaids up the aisle, or bridesmaids and groomsmen may exit separately. The best man either may escort the maid or matron of honor or may exit through a side door and meet the groom in the vestibule.

The parents of the bride and groom traditionally do not participate in the recessional. All members of the congregation remain standing during the recessional.

The Roman Catholic Wedding

Catholic weddings are rarely conducted outside a church. The typical Catholic wedding is a nuptial Mass and takes place in the afternoon or evening. Some Catholic weddings are performed without the Mass.

Most details of the Catholic wedding are similar to those of the Christian wedding described on the preceding pages. A few differences are described below.

During a nuptial Mass, the bride and groom are seated on two chairs or kneel on a prie-dieu before the altar. The maid of honor and the best man remain in the sanctuary with the bride and groom. The other attendants may be seated in the front pews.

The bride and groom are the first to receive Communion, followed by their attendants and parents. Any guests who wish to receive the sacrament may step up to the Communion stations next.

If the bride and groom wish, they may present a bouquet of flowers to the Virgin Mary. The bride and groom together place the bouquet before her statue or on the steps of her altar. A short prayer usually accompanies this ritual.

At the end of the typical Catholic wedding, the priest introduces the newlyweds to the congregation, and the guests respond with applause. The wedding party then genuflect together, and the recessional begins.

The Orthodox Christian Wedding

The beliefs and practices of the Orthodox Christian Church are similar in many ways to those of the Roman Catholic Church, but Orthodox Christians do not acknowledge the Pope as their spiritual leader. Liturgical traditions—including wedding traditions—vary according to the ethnic background of the congregation. (The Greek Orthodox wedding ceremony has not changed since the ninth century!)

The Orthodox Christian wedding ceremony always takes place during the daytime and in church. An a capella choir usually sings. The processional is the same as in any other Christian wedding service. The bride's father gives her away at the altar, then takes a seat beside his wife.

The marriage ceremony is divided into two parts: the Office of Betrothal and the Office of Crowning. The Office of Betrothal takes place first, and its focus is the blessing and exchange of rings, a ritual during which the bride and groom demonstrate that they are joining in marriage of their own free will. The Office of Crowning immediately follows the Office of Betrothal. During the Office of Crowning, the priest places crowns on the heads of the bride and groom. For Greek Orthodox weddings, the crowns are made of leaves and flowers. For Russian Orthodox weddings, the crowns are made of silver and gold. The crowns symbolize both joy and martyrdom, since every true marriage involves self-sacrifice by both partners. At the end of the ceremony, the bride and groom drink from the same cup of wine, which recalls the biblical miracle during the wedding feast at Cana.

The Quaker Wedding

In the Quaker Church (known officially as the Religious Society of Friends), a wedding may take place at home, in a garden, or in a meeting-house. The wedding usually has no officiant. The bride may or may not wear a wedding gown and veil.

At the beginning of the ceremony, the bride and groom may follow the typical Christian processional or simply walk down the aisle together. The couple take seats facing the people. After a period of traditional Quaker silence, anyone who is moved by the Holy Spirit may offer a prayer, a reflection, or good wishes to the bride and groom. The couple then rise, hold hands, and exchange vows. After the bride and groom sit down again, ushers bring a table bearing the Quaker marriage certificate. The certificate is read aloud and signed by the bride, groom, and overseers. It is officially registered later. The regular Quaker meeting follows the wedding ceremony. When the meeting is over, all the people shake hands with those to their right and to their left. All guests sign the marriage certificate before leaving. The marriage certificate is treasured by the bride and groom as a memento of their wedding day.

A Quaker wedding may or may not include music. The reception usually does not include alcoholic beverages.

The Christian Science Wedding

A Christian Science wedding is similar to most Protestant weddings. However, there is no ordained minister in the Christian Science Church who has the authority to perform a marriage ceremony. Therefore, when a Christian Scientist wishes to be married, a minister from any Protestant faith is invited to officiate. The ceremony may take place in the officiant's church or at home. The ceremony is followed by a reception at which no alcoholic beverages are served.

The Mormon Wedding

The members of the Mormon Church (known officially as the Church of Jesus Christ of Latter-Day Saints) practice two kinds of marriage ceremonies.

One ceremony is performed in the temple by the holy priesthood. At this ceremony, the couple is declared wed "for time and for all eternity" instead of "until death do you part." All brides married in the temple dress in white and wear veils, even if they have been married before.

The second kind of marriage ceremony is a civil marriage performed by a bishop of the church or any other accredited person. If the couple comply with the requirements of the church in their daily living, they may be married again in the temple "for time and for all eternity."

The reception is usually held in the cultural hall of the church or in the home of the bride's parents. Because Mormons abstain from alcoholic beverages, none are served at the reception.

The Filipino Wedding

In the traditional Filipino wedding ceremony, which was derived from the practices of eighteenth-century Spanish missionaries, the bride and groom dress in pure white and stand before the altar with several sets of sponsors. The sponsors are reverently referred to as Ninongs (male) and Ninangs (female). The sponsors commit themselves to provide encouragement and guidance to the newlyweds.

For detailed information about the traditional Filipino wedding, consult the book *Kasalan* by Jose Moreno.

The Jewish Wedding

The Jewish religion has three distinct denominations: Orthodox, Conservative, and Reform. Orthodox Judaism adheres most strictly to dietary and other religious laws. Conservative Judaism is less strict, and Reform Judaism is the most lenient. There are many similarities—as well as differences—among the three denominations.

In Orthodox and Conservative synagogues, all men must cover their heads as a sign of respect. For anyone who does not have a hat, a skullcap may be provided in the vestibule. Women, too, usually cover their heads in Orthodox and Conservative synagogues. The bride's family sits on the right side of the aisle, and the groom's family sits on the left side. In some very strict synagogues, men and women are not allowed to sit together. In Reform synagogues, wedding guests are seated with the bride's family on the left and groom's family on the right (the same way as for Christian weddings).

The Processional and Ceremony

In Orthodox and Conservative weddings, the rabbi waits at the altar before the Holy Ark. He stands under a huppah, or flowered canopy, which symbolizes the home that the couple will share. The ushers walk down the aisle in pairs, followed by the bridesmaids (also in pairs) and the best man, who walks alone. The groom then walks down the aisle between his parents, with his mother on his right and his father on his left. (It is also fairly common today for the groom to be waiting at the altar with the best man.) The maid of honor is next in the procession, followed by the flower girl, if any. Finally, the bride walks down the aisle between her parents, with her mother on her right and her father on her left. The bride stands to the groom's right. The bride, groom, best man, and maid of honor stand beneath the huppah with the rabbi. If there is enough room, the fathers or all the parents may also stand beneath the huppah. If there is not enough room under the huppah, the parents stand nearby, each set near their own offspring. If the huppah is particularly roomy, grandparents often participate in both the processional and the ceremony.

In a Reform wedding, the father of the bride escorts his daughter on his right arm down the aisle. The groom, best man, and rabbi wait at the altar. A Reform wedding usually does not include a huppah, although this option is available in many Reform synagogues.

The End of the Ceremony

At the end of the ceremony, in both Orthodox and Conservative synagogues, the groom crushes a wineglass beneath his foot, making a loud noise. This ritual reminds all present of the sacking of the Second Temple of Jerusalem in A.D. 70. Some also believe that the glass-breaking ritual scares away the devil. In a Reform wedding, no ceremonial wineglass is broken. (Again, this option is still available in many Reform synagogues.)

The Recessional

In the Orthodox and Conservative recessional, the bride and groom walk up the aisle first, followed by the bride's parents, the groom's parents, and the attendants. In the Reform recessional, the attendants precede the parents.

Music

At large Orthodox and Conservative weddings, a cantor may be engaged to chant. At any Jewish wedding, musical selections and instrumentation depend on the couple's tastes and the advice of the music director.

The Chinese Wedding

The Engagement Ceremony

The engagement ceremony is a very important event that takes place on a lucky day according to the lunar calendar. During this ceremony the men from the bride and groom's families (including the grandfathers) are seated in a circle, and the bride offers a small cup of tea with both hands to each male member of the groom's family. A small boy is included in the circle for good luck, in hope of assuring the birth of a male child.

The groom's family offers the bride's family a red envelope containing a generous amount of money. This money goes to pay for the wedding feast. (The bride's family does not pay for any part of the wedding feast, but it does provide furniture and appliances for the newlyweds' home.) Any surplus money will be kept by the newlyweds. The bride and groom's parents together choose a lucky wedding date from the lunar calendar.

The Wedding Ceremony and Banquet

The Chinese wedding is a civil ceremony. During the wedding ceremony, the bride's ring may be placed only halfway onto her finger to signify that husband and wife are equal and that one does not rule over the other.

A large red banner embroidered with a dragon for good luck is placed on a table and signed by all the guests. Firecrackers welcome the newlyweds to a huge banquet. The whole of both families and many friends are invited to the banquet. Sometimes as many as one hundred tables of ten guests each attend a wedding, and all the guests bring red envelopes containing gifts of money.

During the course of the wedding day, the bride may wear three or four different dresses. She may wear one dress for the ceremony, a different dress when she enters the banquet, another one as she circulates among the tables and thanks everyone for coming, and yet another one as she stands in the receiving line and gives the guests a box of cookies as they leave.

The Japanese Wedding

Elaborate American-style weddings are popular in Japan, where, as in the United States, many religions are recognized. Christian church chimes, Buddhist bells, and Shinto gongs may be combined to welcome guests to a formal Japanese wedding. Rental boutiques provide both traditional Japanese kimonos and Western dress. The bride and groom may wear both, changing during the ceremony. A simple sip of sake (rice wine) may replace the words "I do." In modern Japan, both sets of parents may help pay for the wedding. Most Japanese newlyweds (78 percent) honeymoon abroad in Australia, Hawaii, New Zealand, or Europe.

The African-American Wedding

Because Americans of African ancestry trace their heritage to many different African cultures, there is no single standard African-American ceremony. There are, however, many similarities among the various ceremonies.

The most widely known African-American wedding custom is called "jumping the broom"— a practice that began during the era of slavery. Neither courts nor churches in the United States recognized slave marriages, but some plantation owners nonetheless allowed their slaves to marry unofficially. At the end of the wedding ceremony, according to slave narratives, the bride and groom jumped over a broom "into the land of matrimony."

The wedding broom is usually made of straw, with a long handle decorated with flowers and ribbon. The bristles may also be covered with a bow or cloth of African design. There are several theories about what the broom represents. In some African cultures, a bride would help her new in-laws sweep their house as a gesture of solidarity. In some African and European cultures, a broom was a symbol of domesticity. In southern Europe, giving a broom to newlyweds was supposed to bring them good luck. Historians suggest that slaves may have combined both European and African influences to create this distinctly African-American ritual.

Jumping the broom is a way of commemorating the way in which African ancestors may have been married. Some clergy do not allow this ritual to be part of a church service. If this is the case, the ritual may be performed at the reception, before the first dance.

For more information on African-American wedding traditions, please refer to Harriete Cole's book *Jumping the Broom: The African-American Wedding Planner.*

The Baha'i Wedding

A prerequisite for marriage in the Baha'i faith is to obtain parental consent, which is presented in writing to the local spiritual assembly. This is followed by a public statement in the presence of two witnesses, who may be chosen either by the assembly or by the couple. The couple pledge their troth by saying, "We will all verily abide by the will of God."

There is no prescribed ritual for a Baha'i wedding ceremony. Much individual thought goes into it, and the result is described for guests in a wedding program. The ceremony may include readings from Baha'i scripture and the scripture of other faiths. Music and flowers are permitted.

The Ecumenical or Interfaith Wedding

When the bride and groom are of different faiths, the wedding may be held in either of their churches, at home, or in any appropriate location. Two clergymembers—one from each faith—may co-officiate. One may read the vows, for example, and the other may offer a blessing.

In order to avoid misunderstandings, confusion, or duplication of rites, prayers, or sentiments, an interfaith ceremony should be carefully planned and tactfully discussed with both officiants.

For More Information

For more information on weddings in any of the religious or ethnic traditions described on the preceding pages, or for information on traditions not covered in this book, contact Lois A. Pearce, Master Bridal Consultant and author of *Ethnic and Specialty Wedding Guide,* at The Association of Bridal Consultants, 200 Chestnutland Road, New Milford, Connecticut 06776-2521.

Another excellent book is Shu Shu Costa's Asian-American wedding planner titled *Wild Geese and Tea.* This book details the origins and practices of Chinese, Japanese, and Korean weddings.

Notes

Notes

Chapter Sixteen

The
Wedding Day

*Marriage is that relation between man and woman
in which independence is equal, the dependence
is mutual, and the obligation is reciprocal.*

LOUIS KAUFMAN ANSPACHER

On your wedding day, you will awake with the delicious knowledge that when you and your beloved return to sleep that evening, you will be husband and wife. Focus on the happy, long-awaited event that's about to happen, and rest assured that your careful planning will make it happen without a hitch.

To help you fully enjoy every precious moment of this day, think through the entire sequence of events that will take place so that nothing is overlooked or forgotten. On the pages that follow, you'll find a brief description of each part of a typical wedding day, followed by a sample wedding-weekend schedule.

Assembling and Preparing

It is easy to assemble the wedding party for a home wedding, because the members who live there are already present. The rest of the party usually dress at home and assemble at the ceremony site or at the home or lodgings of another member of the wedding party.

When the ceremony takes place elsewhere—in a church, hotel, or club, for example—it may be more convenient to have everyone meet and dress at the ceremony site. Whether this is possible depends on the facilities and transportation available, the time of day, the number of people involved, and the temperaments of those people. Some prefer to prepare for a big event in private, and such preferences should be respected.

Regardless of where the members of the wedding party assemble, consider providing a tray of sandwiches for them. People tend to be too busy and excited to eat right before a wedding, yet without some nourishment, they may not have enough energy to enjoy the full day ahead. The thoughtful provision of a snack is sure to inspire gratitude and may even prevent fainting spells.

After the wedding party has assembled as directed, the attendants review their instructions for the day and offer to help the bride and groom with any last-minute personal preparations. Everyone supports and compliments the bride and groom, and they, in turn, thank everyone for being so kind, loving, and helpful.

If a makeup artist and hairstylist have been hired, they complete their work well before the ceremony is scheduled to begin. The florist is arranging flowers and delivering bouquets and boutonnieres. Now is a good time for a photographer to take candid photos.

If the ceremony is being held outdoors, the tent and chairs are set up. The area is sprayed for flies, mosquitoes, and other pesky insects.

At this time the caterer is preparing refreshments, the musicians are arranging equipment and warming up, and the officiant is reviewing his or her notes. Before long, the guests will be arriving—and all systems are go!

At the Ceremony Site

The following paragraphs describe the sequence of events for a traditional church wedding. The sequence can and should be adapted for a ceremony that will be less traditional or that will take place at a different type of site.

The First to Arrive

The ushers arrive at the church from forty-five minutes to an hour before the ceremony and wait in the vestibule to seat guests.

The groom and best man arrive about thirty minutes before the ceremony and enter the church by a side door. They wait in the clergymember's study or in the vestry until they receive a signal that the ceremony is about to begin.

The bride and groom's parents and the remaining attendants arrive at least fifteen minutes before the ceremony. They wait in the vestibule with the ushers.

Seating Parents

When the parents and attendants are all assembled, an usher escorts the groom's mother to the right front pew. The groom's father follows right behind them. The last person seated by an usher is the bride's mother. She is escorted to the left front pew. If any guests arrive after the mother of the bride has been seated, they should slip unobtrusively into rear pews.

When parents are divorced and remarried, the mother and stepfather sit in the front pew. The father and stepmother sit in the second pew. If a divorced parent has not remarried, he or she may choose to sit with a close relative or friend.

If an adopted bride or groom has invited a biological parent to the wedding, the adoptive parents are seated in the front pew. The biological parent may be seated in the second or third pew.

Aisle Runner and Ribbons

When a white aisle runner is used, two ushers unroll it from the front of the church toward the rear to cover the entire length of the main aisle. When the runner is in place, the ushers may fasten a long, broad white ribbon to the last reserved pew on each side of the aisle and unroll the ribbons from the front of the church toward the rear, draping them over the end of each pew. These ribbons remain in place until the family and friends in the reserved pews leave the church after the ceremony. The rest of the guests are then dismissed one row at a time by the ushers.

The Processional

The bride and her father arrive at the church just as the ceremony is about to start. The procession forms in the vestibule. When signaled, the officiant, the groom, and the best man assume their places at the front of the church. The processional then begins.

At the Altar

The members of the wedding party stand in their designated places. When the bride reaches the groom's side, she releases her father's arm and takes the groom's arm. Alternatively, the couple may hold hands or simply stand side by side.

The Ceremony

At this point, the ceremony begins. Because wedding ceremonies vary so much, I will not attempt to provide a play-by-play description. However, I will discuss below a few common components that often raise logistical questions.

The Bride's Bouquet

The typical wedding ceremony includes at least one part during which the bride and groom need both hands free. They may, for example, face each other and hold hands while reciting their vows, light a unity candle, and/or place rings on each other's fingers. If the ceremony includes any such rituals, the bride should hand her bouquet to her maid of honor, who can hand the bouquet back to the bride before the recessional.

The Exchange of Rings

An engaged woman usually wears her engagment ring on the ring finger of her left hand. That is also the finger on which the wedding ring is usually worn, so how does the bride manage these two rings on her wedding day? She should transfer her engagement ring to the ring finger of her right hand before the ceremony. During the ceremony, the groom places her wedding ring on the ring finger of her left hand. After the ceremony, the bride transfers her engagement ring to the ring finger of her left hand, above her wedding ring. (Custom suggests that the bride wear her wedding ring nearest to her heart.)

The Kiss

If the ceremony includes a kiss at the end, and the bride is wearing a veil with a blusher, the maid of honor lifts the blusher before the bride turns to kiss the groom. Then the recessional begins.

The Recessional

The bride and groom are the first to walk up the aisle smiling happily at the guests. Sometimes the bride stops to give her mother a flower and her father a kiss. The newlyweds are followed by their attendants in the order they've rehearsed.

Next, the ushers approach the reserved pews and escort the parents and honored guests to the vestibule. They then remove the white ribbons, if used, and dismiss the guests pew by pew starting from the front of the church.

After the Ceremony

Formal Photographs

A photographer usually takes pictures of the newlyweds as they proceed up the aisle and as they emerge from the church. Sometimes the couple and the wedding party pose for formal pictures before leaving for the reception. However, if the photographer is slow, this arrangement can substantially delay the reception. Many couples avoid this problem by having formal photographs taken either before the ceremony or after guests have gone through the receiving line at the reception. If the photographer is not shooting formals right after the ceremony, he or she is then free to go directly to the reception site and take shots of the decorations and the cake—before guests arrive to obstruct his or her view of the room.

Wedding Bells

Borrow a joyous English custom and let the church bells peal after the ceremony! This may be arranged through the clergyperson or an assistant.

At the Reception Site

The Receiving Line

Regardless of the size or formality of a wedding, guests will want to greet the bride and groom personally and wish them well. A receiving line allows the guests to do so in a graceful manner.

Choosing a Location

Wedding guests traditionally proceed through a receiving line at the reception. Choose the location for your receiving line carefully to avoid creating a bottleneck. It is much better to choose in advance than to let a spontaneous line form in a spot that blocks an entrance or exit. Allow plenty of room for a smooth, quick flow of guests, and position the receiving line so that guests may, if necessary, deposit coats, hats, boots, umbrellas, and so on before approaching the line.

A Mother Receives

The traditional receiving line starts with the bride's mother, followed by the groom's mother. (This arrangement presumes that the wedding is taking place in the bride's hometown.) If the wedding is held in the groom's hometown, and his mother knows most of the guests by sight, it is better for her to be first in line so she can greet guests by name.

The two fathers may either stand in the receiving line next to their wives or mingle with guests. If the fathers choose to mingle, they should do so together so that they can introduce each other if necessary.

The groom stands next to the parents, followed by the bride. The maid or matron of honor stands next to the bride. Because she is the last person in the receiving line, she graciously directs guests to the refreshment area. If anyone in the receiving line is wearing gloves, the gloves may be kept on or taken off, as the wearer wishes.

The other members of the wedding party usually do not stand in the receiving line, because too many people slow down the process. (Young children are never expected to stand in a receiving line.) Bridesmaids and groomsmen should mingle with the guests in a friendly way.

At a very large, formal wedding, an announcer may stand at the beginning of the receiving line. The announcer asks each guest for his or her name and repeats the name to the first mother in line in case the mother and the guest have not yet met.

It is not necessary to make clever conversation in the receiving line. Parents should welcome guests to the celebration. The bride and groom should tell guests how glad they are to see them. Guests should congratulate the groom and offer best wishes to the bride. (Traditionally, the bride is not congratulated; this custom helps guests avoid implying that the bride has "snared" a husband.) Guests should introduce themselves if necessary, make a brief complimentary remark, and move on.

When there are many guests and a long line, it is perfectly acceptable for a guest to enjoy a glass of champagne and circulate until the receiving line shortens. Guests should place their empty glasses on a table before proceeding through the line.

A Father Receives

If the bride or groom's father is hosting the wedding but is not married, he stands first in the receiving line. He may also invite an aunt, grandmother, or other female relative to receive with him.

Stepparents and Biological Parents

If the bride or groom's parents are divorced and remarried, the stepparents do not stand in the receiving line unless they are hosting the wedding.

If the bride or groom is adopted and a biological parent has been invited to the wedding, the biological parent does not stand in the receiving line. He or she is introduced to guests as a friend of the family.

The Bride and Groom Receive

When the bride and groom host a small, informal wedding, they may receive the guests together by standing at the exit of the ceremony site or at the entrance to the reception site. The maid or matron of honor may stand near the bride and groom and direct guests to the refreshment area.

No Receiving Line

If a wedding is very large, with hundreds of guests in attendance, it may be better to simply omit the receiving line. If there will be no receiving line, the two sets of parents may station themselves in separate parts of the room and greet the guests informally. The bride and groom should make every effort to circulate among the guests and have a friendly word with everyone. Alternatively, a warm welcome may be extended over the public-address system.

The Guest Book

The guest book is placed on a table near the entrance to the reception or at the end of the receiving line. A plumed pen usually accompanies the book and helps call attention to it. It is also helpful to station a family member, friend, or attendant near the guest book to remind each guest to sign it. The guest book will become a treasured memento of the wedding day.

Gifts

Some guests will bring gifts to the reception, so a table for these gifts should be made available. The table should be in a secure place near the entrance. It is wise to assign someone the honor of supervising the gift table and transporting the gifts and cards from the reception site to the newlyweds' future home.

Seating

The Informal Reception

Chairs and tables are provided, and the guests sit wherever they please. Refreshments are made available, a little music fills the air, and the best man proposes the first toast. The wedding cake is the highlight of the reception. When it is time to cut the cake, the guests are notified and all gather around to watch.

The Formal Reception

Customs vary in different parts of the United States, but usually when a reception includes a seated meal, a head table is placed in a prominent position facing the rest of the tables. The bride and groom sit in the center of the head table, with the bride on the right and the groom on the left. The maid or matron of honor sits to the groom's left, and the best man sits to the bride's right. The rest of the attendants (and possibly their spouses, too) are seated in the remaining chairs at the head table, alternating men and women as much as possible.

One or more reserved tables may be positioned near the head table. The parents of the bride and groom, the officiant and his or her spouse, and close relatives and friends of the bride and groom may be seated at reserved tables.

An alternative arrangement is to seat the bride and groom, the officiant and spouse, the parents and grandparents, and the best man and maid or matron of honor at the head table. The remaining members of the wedding party are then seated at reserved tables near the head table.

The bride and groom are seated at the head table either just before or just after the reserved tables are seated. The newlyweds may be introduced to the strains of "Here Comes the Bride" or other wedding music. A blessing may be said before the meal is served. Waitstaff may serve the head table and reserved tables even if the rest of the guests serve themselves at a buffet.

Place Cards

Place cards are helpful tools that prevent indecision and/or confusion over where to sit at a reception. They are particularly useful for seating guests in congenial groups at very large formal receptions. Even if place cards are not used for all the guests, they are always used at the head table and reserved tables.

Place cards should be written legibly in dark green, blue, brown, or black ink (avoid light-colored or metallic inks) so they are easy to read without glasses even in soft candlelight. On informal place cards, the first name only or the first and last name are written: "William" or "William Baldwin." On formal place cards, the full name is written: "Mr. William Baldwin." The place card should be positioned directly above the dinner plate at each place setting.

When guests arrive at the door, they pick up envelopes labeled with their names. Table numbers are written on small cards inside the envelopes. Guests then locate their tables and sit in their assigned places. Usually couples are assigned to the same table but are not seated next to each other. A table for eight might include two couples who know each other and two additional couples they might enjoy meeting.

Seating need not be assigned until the day before the wedding, as there are always last-minute cancellations and additions. It takes about one to two hours to arrange congenial seating for approximately 150 people.

Dancing

When a reception includes dancing, the leader of the band or the disc jockey often announces the beginning of the wedding dance formalities. Alternatively, a member of the wedding party may assume this role.

The First Dance

At a formal reception, the bride and groom usually start the dancing after the first course has been served. The first dance usually follows this sequence: (1) The bride and groom dance the first dance together. (2) The bride's father cuts in on the groom and dances with the bride. (3) The groom asks the bride's mother to dance. (4) The groom's father cuts in on the bride's father and dances with the bride. (5) The bride's father cuts in on the groom and dances with the bride's mother. (6) The groom asks his mother to dance. (7) After a few minutes, the announcer invites all the guests to dance.

When parents are divorced or widowed, there are no guidelines for the first dance besides common sense.

Ethnic Dances

The hora is an Israeli folk dance often performed at weddings. The guests hold hands and form a circle around the newlyweds. The newlyweds hold a linen napkin between them as they are lifted up on chairs and the guests dance around them.

In the Greek handkerchief dance, the groom is linked to the bride by a handkerchief while other dancers line up, holding each other's shoulders, and weave around the room.

The tarantella is a lively Italian folk dance with quick hops and tapping foot movements.

To dance the Grand March, the newlyweds link arms and lead their attendants and guests around the room and sometimes outside. They then form an arch with their arms, and the guests pass under in pairs. After passing under, each pair stops and forms another arch under which the remaining dancers pass. This continues until all the dancers have passed under the arches. Starting with the last pair of dancers to form an arch, the line then disbands pair by pair. Each pair passes under the arches in reverse, kissing the newlyweds as they emerge. The dance ends when the newlyweds are at the head of the line again. (They may, of course, repeat the sequence if they wish!)

The dollar dance is an old Polish custom that requires men who dance with the bride to fill her purse with money or pin bills to her veil. It is still popular in some communities.

Toasting

At a reception that includes a seated meal, traditionally the best man rises and makes the first toast to the newlyweds as soon as all the guests have been served and their glasses have been filled with wine or sparkling beverage. The best man mentions the bride and groom by name, states his relationship with them, and offers them his wish for their future. He is followed by the groom, who stands and thanks the best man, welcomes the guests, toasts the bride for his good fortune, and thanks both families for their support. If she wishes, the bride then rises and offers a brief toast to her groom and to both families. Her toast is followed by toasts from both fathers or from other members of the wedding party. After the wedding party has finished, anyone may offer a toast.

The best time to offer a toast is between courses. At a large gathering, a person proposing a toast usually stands. At a small gathering, he or she remains seated and merely raises a glass. A toast should be brief, loving, and in good taste. The person toasted remains seated, listens attentively, and accepts the toast with a nod or a slight bow. When the newlyweds are toasted, they look at each other before raising their glasses and sipping from them. Guests usually remain seated during a toast, but they may choose to stand when a toast is proposed to the newlyweds. Guests seated at a table together should be sure to make eye contact with each other while participating in a toast. If there is no wine left in one's glass, one may simply raise the empty glass and pretend to take a sip. If no wineglass is available, the water glass is raised. Clinking of glasses while toasting is optional.

Following are some toasts appropriate for weddings:

"May you live as long as you want, and may you never want as long as you live." —Unknown

"Here's to the groom with bride so fair, and here's to the bride with groom so rare!" —Unknown

"May you grow old on one pillow." —Old Armenian toast

"To the triumph of hope over experience." —Samuel Johnson

"You only get married for the second time once." —Garrison Keillor

"Love, be true to her.

Life, be dear to her.

Health, stay close to her.

Joy, draw near to her.

Fortune, find what you can do for her;

search your treasure-house through for her;

follow her footsteps the wide world over;

and keep her husband always her lover!"

　　—Old English toast

Tapping Glasses

In some communities it is customary for guests to tap their glasses with silverware, which signals the bride and groom to kiss. Sometimes guests get carried away with this custom; if they do, the bride and groom can simply smile and wave.

Cutting the Wedding Cake

The wedding cake may be placed as a centerpiece on the head table or the buffet table, or it may be displayed on its own special table draped elegantly with a fancy lace or embroidered tablecloth.

For a tea or cocktail reception, the wedding cake is cut just after all the guests have been received. At a reception that includes a seated meal, the wedding cake is cut just before dessert is served. Usually a photographer is directed to take pictures as the bride, with the groom's hand over hers, cuts the first two slices. The groom offers the bride a bite of the first slice, and the bride offers the groom a bite of the second slice.

A designated person then steps in to continue cutting the cake, which is served to all the guests. It is thoughtful to serve first any children who are present. (If individual boxes of groom's cake or truffles will be provided as favors, guests pick these up as they leave the reception, not at cake-cutting time, dessert time, or any other time during the reception.)

The cake should be cut with a thin, sharp, serrated silver or porcelain cake knife. (An ordinary kitchen knife will not show up well in a photograph.) A second utensil called a server is also needed so that the cake cutter can avoid using his or her fingers when transferring slices of cake onto plates. If frosting sticks to the knife, it should be wiped off with a clean, damp paper towel after each slice is cut.

To cut a round, three-tiered wedding cake, start with the bottom tier. Cut medium-sized slices around the outside of the bottom tier, up to the edge of the middle tier. When this step is completed, cut slices from the middle tier in the same manner. Now return to cutting the newly exposed section of the bottom tier. Remove the top tier (which is traditionally frozen and eaten by the newlyweds upon their return from their honeymoon or at their one-month or one-year anniversary), separate the remaining portions of the bottom and middle tiers, and cut these into slices.

Tossing the Bouquet and Garter

The tossing of the bouquet and garter may occur either before or after the bride and groom change into their traveling clothes. The newlyweds signal the maid or matron of honor and the best man to gather all the single men and women. Then the bride tosses a bouquet over her shoulder to the women. Tradition says that the woman who catches it will become the next bride. Next, the groom tosses the bride's garter to the bachelors. Tradition says that the man who catches it will become the next groom.

The Newlyweds' Departure

Before leaving the reception, the bride and groom thank their attendants individually, if they haven't already done so, and say good-bye to their parents privately. As the bride and groom leave for their car, they may be showered with flower petals and good wishes for a long life of married bliss.

Wedding-Weekend Checklist

A wedding-weekend checklist that includes a schedule and summary of events can give the bride and groom a reassuring feeling of control and can help everyone involved keep the events running smoothly. I recommend making many photocopies of your checklist, color-coding them, and sharing them with everyone involved—from family members to attendants to hired help such as caterers, florists, photographers, and musicians.

Following is a sample checklist for a 7:00 P.M. church wedding followed by a buffet dinner. When you write up your checklist, simply insert the appropriate times, places, and names for your wedding.

Wedding of Jennifer Lovejoy and William Baldwin

Friday, June 9, 2000

Rehearsal
Time: 6:00 P.M.
Place: Basilica of Saint Mary
Address: 88 North Seventeenth Street, Minneapolis, Minnesota

Rehearsal Dinner
Time: 7:00 P.M.
Place: Loring Café
Address: 1624 Harmon Place, Minneapolis, Minnesota
Hosts: Mr. and Mrs. Richard Baldwin

Memo to Jennifer and William: Bring packed traveling clothes, guest book and pen, reception favors, programs, and maps for designated people to bring to reception site. Bring wedding rings, marriage license, and officiant's fee for maid of honor and best man to bring to ceremony. Bring attendants' gifts.

Saturday, June 10, 2000

Ceremony
Time: 7:00 P.M.
Place: Basilica of Saint Mary
Address: 88 North Seventeenth Street, Minneapolis, Minnesota

Reception
Time: 8:00 P.M.
Place: Minneapolis Athletic Club
Address: 615 Second Avenue South, Minneapolis, Minnesota

Preceremony Schedule
4:30 P.M.: Jennifer and her family and attendants meet, dressed, at the Lovejoy home. (A tray of light sandwiches will be provided.) Florist delivers bouquets, corsages, headpieces, and boutonniere for Mr. Lovejoy. *Memo to maid of honor:* Bring marriage license and William's wedding ring.

4:45 P.M.: Photographer takes candids at Lovejoy home.

5:00 P.M.: Florist delivers to church flower arrangements plus boutonnieres and corsages for William and his family and attendants. Caterer begins preparations at reception site.

5:30 P.M.: Ushers arrive at church, pin on boutonnieres, and review instructions regarding programs, maps, and seating.

6:00 P.M.: William and his family and attendants arrive at church. Three cars will be available at Lovejoy home. *Memo to best man:* Bring officiant's fee and Jennifer's wedding ring.

6:10 P.M.: Photographer arrives at church and takes candids of William and his family and attendants. Florist delivers flowers to reception site.

6:15 P.M.: Musicians arrive at church. Car one leaves Lovejoy home with bridesmaids. Car two leaves Lovejoy home with maid of honor, grandparents, and Mrs. Lovejoy.

6:20 P.M.: Car three leaves Lovejoy home with Jennifer and Mr. Lovejoy.

6:30 P.M.: Ushers hand out programs and seat guests. Prelude music begins.

6:40 P.M.: Entire wedding party waits in church vestibule. Altar candles are lit.

6:50 P.M.: Ushers seat Mrs. Baldwin and William's grandparents.

6:58 P.M.: Usher seats Mrs. Lovejoy.

7:00 P.M.: Solo is sung.

7:05 P.M.: Ceremony begins.

Post-Ceremony Schedule

7:30 P.M.: Valet parking attendants arrive at reception site.

7:45 P.M.: Reception musicians are ready to play, caterer is finishing food preparations, bar is open, and waitstaff are prepared to serve champagne on trays as guests arrive at reception. Car one transports Jennifer and William to reception. Car two transports Jennifer and William's parents and grandparents to reception. Car three transports bridesmaids to reception. Best man escorts maid of honor to reception in his car. Groomsmen and ushers escort guests without transportation to reception.

7:50 P.M.: Receiving line forms.

Reception Schedule

8:00 P.M.: Hors d'oeuvres are passed.

8:30 P.M.: Photographer takes formal photographs of wedding party.

8:45 P.M.: Jennifer and William begin the traditional first dance.

9:00 P.M.: Buffet supper is served.

9:30 P.M.: Jennifer, William, and best man proceed to cake table. Three glasses of champagne are waiting there. Best man proposes a toast and others follow suit. Jennifer and William cut the first slice of cake as photographer takes photos. Waitstaff cut and serve cake to guests.

10:15 P.M.: Best man announces tossing of bouquet and garter, and he and maid of honor assemble single men and women. After tossing ceremony, Jennifer and William leave reception to change clothes, then return to say good-bye. Bridesmaids distribute flower petals to guests for showering the newlyweds as they depart. *Memo to family and attendants:* After Jennifer and William's departure, gather their wedding attire, top tier of wedding cake, guest book, flowers, and gifts, and transport to a designated place. Thank caterer and musicians. Return rented wedding clothes.

After the Wedding

If the wedding takes place during the day, family and friends may wish to congregate in little groups afterward to review and savor the day's events.

Dear Edith,

Not much has been written about what needs to be done after a wedding reception besides waving the bride and groom off on their honeymoon. Do you have a list of things to do after the wedding?

ANSWER: Indeed I do! (1) Someone must transport the wedding gifts home from the reception site. (2) Someone must pay the caterer, the musicians, and any other help hired for the reception. (3) Someone must check and count borrowed or rented equipment (chairs, tables, coffeemakers, linens, silver, china, glassware, and so on) and see that everything is returned in good order. (4) If the reception was not catered, someone must deal with the food platters. (5) Someone must check on the alcoholic beverages and return unopened bottles for credit. (6) Someone must decide who is to receive the flower arrangements, centerpieces, or other decorations. (7) Someone must pick up the guest book. (8) Someone must make sure that nothing has been left behind by any guest. (9) Someone must see that there is proper transportation available for the cleanup crew and equipment. (10) Someone must ensure that everyone is properly thanked. (11) Someone must return the rental suits, shoes, and so on to the rental store. (12) Someone must take the bride's gown to a dry cleaner as soon as possible to be cleaned and preserved. (13) If announcements are to be sent, someone must mail them immediately after the wedding. (Do not wait until after the honeymoon.) (14) Someone must ensure that all of the above is done in good order.

Such a gathering may take place in a kitchen, around a swimming pool, or even while driving to the airport. If the wedding takes place in the evening, an informal afterglow may be planned for the day after the wedding. (Please refer to Chapter Two for specific suggestions for informal parties.)

Regardless of where or when it happens, reminiscing can be one of the most heartwarming experiences of the entire wedding weekend. Who wouldn't enjoy a chuckle over the near-disaster that happened when Grandmother was forgotten at the beauty parlor and almost missed the wedding? Who wouldn't become misty-eyed remembering the unexpected tears of the groom's father at the rehearsal? Who wouldn't sigh with relief and gratitude recalling the choirboy who cleverly jimmied open the car door for the bride's mother, who had locked her keys inside? Who wouldn't laugh out loud recalling the hilarious scene when a puppy ran off with the flower girl's shoe?

If the newlyweds plan a delayed honeymoon, they may even share in the reminiscing, watch their wedding video in the company of loved ones, and open gifts that were brought to the reception.

A casual, shoes-off gathering helps everyone unwind and provides an essential transition back to everyday life for those who have spent so much time and energy on the wedding.

Parting Words for the Bride and Groom

After all your guests have gone home, your gifts have been put away, and your honeymoon has drawn to a close, you will embark in earnest on your lifelong journey together. I offer you the following words as you set out on the road:

"Sing and dance together and be joyous, but let each one of you be alone,
Even as the strings of a lute are alone though they quiver
  with the same music....
And stand together yet not too near together:
For the pillars of the temple stand apart,
And the oak tree and the cypress grow not in each other's shadow."
—Kahlil Gibran, *The Prophet*

Notes

Notes

Appendix A: Wedding Customs

Why do brides wear white? Why does the best man dress like the groom? Who started the curious practice of throwing rice at weddings? Why do the bride and groom find it necessary to sneak away after the wedding? And why do people play practical jokes on newlyweds?

The Evolution of Wedding Customs

In tracing the evolution of wedding customs, we find that the practice of marriage has progressed through three main stages. In the first stage, marriages were accomplished by force. A man would capture a desirable woman, often from another community. A fellow warrior might help the groom capture and carry off the bride.

Marriage practices then evolved into a second stage, during which marriages were accomplished by contract or purchase. In England, this stage lasted as late as the middle of the sixteenth century. In fact, the Anglo-Saxon word *wed* originally referred to money (or its equivalent in horses, cattle, or other property) the groom paid the father of the bride to seal the marriage contract.

Marriage by mutual love and consent evolved gradually. For a time during the Roman Republic, weddings were solemn religious occasions. During the Roman Empire, however, religion fell into contempt and marriage became virtually a civil contract. As Christianity gained a foothold in the Western world, it slowly gave religious character back to the practice of marriage. At first, couples simply paired off and asked for the blessing of their parish priests. It was not until the Council of Trent, which ended in 1563, that the Catholic Church made it mandatory for a marriage to be performed by a priest in the presence of two or three witnesses. Marriage was regarded as a divine institution throughout Europe until the French Revolution. France's new constitution made civil marriage mandatory in 1791.

Wedding Customs

The Honeymoon

The practice of traveling on a honeymoon after the wedding harks back to the days when a groom often stole his bride and found it necessary to hide her until her family grew tired of searching for her. While in hiding (for about one month—the time it takes for the moon to progress through all its phases), the newlyweds are believed to have drunk wine mixed with honey.

Over the Threshold

The custom of the groom carrying the bride over the threshold may also have originated when marriages were conquests.

Alternatively, some scholars assert that this is a good-luck custom possibly originating with the Romans, who believed that evil spirits dwelt within the threshold. The bride was carried over the threshold to prevent her from stepping on it or tripping over it, thus angering the spirits and releasing them into the newlyweds' home.

The Bridal Veil

The Romans believed that evil spirits were jealous of people's happiness. Since weddings were joyful events, it was necessary to confuse the spirits. Brides wore veils to disguise themselves and throw the evil spirits off their track.

The bridal veil has also served a custom dictating that the bride and groom should not see each other before their wedding. This custom originated when marriages were arranged by the bride and groom's families. The bride and groom did not see each other clearly until they had recited their vows. Then the veil was lifted, and it was too late to back out!

Dressing Alike

The custom of having members of the wedding party dress alike also originated from a belief that evil spirits might wish to harm the bride and groom. The bride and groom surrounded themselves with friends dressed like them in order to deceive the spirits.

Teasing

It was considered dangerous for lovers to be happy, but if evil spirits could be convinced that mortals were truly miserable, it was believed they would consider it a waste of energy to add any supernatural punishments. For this reason, friends and family would often tease the bride and groom, hide their belongings, and make them targets for friendly abuse. Such teasing is still practiced today with the shivaree, a noisy mock serenade held late during the wedding night to harass the newlyweds. The French people of Canada and Louisiana introduced this custom to the United States.

Throwing Rice

If all other efforts to confuse, distract, or deceive evil spirits failed, it was believed possible to buy off the cantankerous creatures by throwing a few handfuls of rice.

It is also believed that throwing rice (or other grains) at newlyweds encouraged them to be fruitful and multiply.

The Engagement Ring

Giving a ring to seal an important or sacred agreement is a very old custom, as demonstrated by this passage from the Old Testament book of Genesis: "And Pharaoh said unto Joseph, 'See, I have set thee over all the land of Egypt.' And Pharaoh took off his ring from his hand, and put it upon Joseph's hand." A Greek betrothal ring recovered from the fourth century B.C. bears the following inscription: "To her who excels not only in virtue and prudence, but also in wisdom."

The Trousseau and Hope Chest

Many young women all over the world collect clothing, linens, household goods, and family treasures in anticipation of their marriage. This collection is called a trousseau. The word *trousseau* originated from the Old French word *trousse* and the Middle English word *trusse,* both of which mean "bundle." A bride stores her trousseau in a hope chest, which traditionally was a wooden chest but may in fact be any type of chest, box, or drawer set aside for this purpose.

The practice of collecting a trousseau in a hope chest grew out of the ancient dowry system. In some cultures, a bride was required to bring a certain amount of money or property to her husband at marriage to be used for setting up housekeeping. The dowry system, in turn, grew out of the much older custom of marriage by purchase.

Courting by Native North Americans

Among Native North Americans, it was customary for a young man to present gifts not to his prospective bride, but to her father. If the gifts were accepted, the betrothal was considered sealed.

Circumcision

Circumcision is a spiritually significant surgical procedure performed on males that is practiced among Jews, Muslims, Christians, many African peoples, the aborigines of Australia, Madagascans, Melanesians, the peoples of the Indian Archipelago, Polynesians, and many Native Americans. Circumcision is considered to be the oldest surgical procedure—it dates back about six thousand years—and is the only procedure with religious significance that is still widely practiced. In some cultures, it is considered a prerequisite for marriage.

Bundling

Bundling, an old New England custom introduced by the Dutch and the English, permitted engaged couples to lie in bed together without undressing during long, cold winter evenings.

Spooning

In Wales, a man would often carve a wooden spoon with his pocketknife and give the spoon to his prospective bride. The woman would attach a ribbon to the spoon and wear it around her neck as a sign of her engagement to the man. The word *spooning*, which means "engaging in amorous behavior," originated from this custom.

The Marriage Season

In Morocco, marriages are generally celebrated in autumn, at the close of the harvest season, when granaries are full. Most European countries follow the Roman tradition of holding weddings in spring, when homage was paid to Ceres, the goddess of agriculture, and Flora, the goddess of flowers.

The Bachelor Party

The custom of the bachelor party is believed to have originated in Sparta, a city in ancient Greece, where the groom entertained his friends at supper on the eve of his wedding. This event was known as the "men's mess."

The Wedding Ring

The wedding ring is believed to have evolved from the engagement ring. The earliest record of wedding-ring symbolism appears in Egyptian hieroglyphics, in which a circle represents eternity. Early Hebrew wedding rings were usually made of plain gold, silver, or base metal with no setting. Even wood, rush, and leather were sometimes used. Apparently, early Jewish wedding rings were of a ceremonial nature because they were often too large to wear on the finger. The use of wedding rings among Christians has been traced back to the year A.D. 860. It is said that when a marriage was properly sealed, rings bearing the names of the newlyweds were passed around for inspection by the wedding guests.

The custom of wearing the wedding ring on the third finger of the left hand grew from the belief that this finger connected directly to the heart via the *vena amoris,* or "vein of love." However, wedding rings have been worn on most fingers of both hands throughout history. Oil paintings of Elizabethan ladies show that during the Elizabethan period in England, a wedding ring was worn on the thumb. In traditional Jewish weddings, the wedding ring is placed on the first finger of the left hand.

The Bridal Gown

Long ago, the typical bride simply wore her best dress on her wedding day. Anne of Brittany, who married Louis XII of France in the late fifteenth century, was the first bride known to have worn an all-white, once-in-a-lifetime bridal gown. Empress Eugénie, a historical fashion leader, introduced the bridal gown as we know it today. She wore a white gown at her wedding to Napoleon III, who ruled France from 1852 to 1871. Many believe that Queen Victoria, who ruled England 1837–1901, is responsible for the popularity of the bridal gown.

The Bridal Wreath

The Crusaders introduced to Europe the custom of wearing a wreath of orange blossoms as a symbol of fertility. Orange blossoms were also carried by brides in their bouquets or worn on their dresses.

In Norway, a bride traditionally wears a wreath of white flowers. After the wedding ceremony, she is blindfolded and surrounded by a circle of bridesmaids. She then dances a folk dance alone and gives the wreath to one of the bridesmaids, who, according to legend, will be the next to wed. The bridesmaid who receives the wreath steps out of the circle, and the bride then hands the wreath to another bridesmaid. The game continues until the last bridesmaid receives the wreath.

Good-Luck Customs

Many brides believe that they should wear "something old, something new, something borrowed, and something blue" on their wedding day. This custom is intended to help create harmony in married life. The wedding day marks the end of an old life and the beginning of a new life, so something old and something new are worn together to symbolize and ease the transition. The borrowed item preferably belongs to a happily married woman, for good luck, and the blue item represents fidelity.

Another popular good-luck custom is the distribution of sugar-coated almonds (wrapped in tulle and tied with ribbon) to wedding guests. This favor, called *confetti* by Italians, represents the bitterness and sweetness of life.

Wedding Cake

Long ago, wedding guests would break biscuits (made of grain, a symbol of fertility) over a bride's head to ensure her fruitfulness. The biscuit crumbs were considered lucky, so guests kept them. Biscuits evolved into buns, which were stacked high by wedding guests. If a bride and groom were able to kiss over the top of the stack, they were ensured many offspring. In order to facilitate stacking, bakers began icing the buns. These fancy pastries evolved into the modern wedding cake. The earlier customs are still evident in some modern practices, such as providing neatly boxed pieces of the groom's cake for guests to take home with them, and saving the top tier of the wedding cake to be eaten on an anniversary.

Toasting

Toasting comes from a French custom of placing a piece of bread in the bottom of a wineglass. Wedding guests shared the wine, and the person who drained the glass to reach the bread received good luck.

Giving Away the Bride

The custom of "giving away" the bride to the groom at the beginning of the wedding ceremony harks back to the days when marriages were considered contracts or purchases. Many modern women find this custom archaic and offensive, yet still wish to acknowledge the important role of parents in the bride and groom's lives. An affectionate alternative to the traditional question "Who gives this woman in holy matrimony?" is the pledge of parents. The pledge below is quoted from the *United Methodist Service of Christian Marriage*:

> PARENTS: We rejoice in your union, and pray God's blessing upon you.
> PEOPLE: In the name of Jesus Christ we love you. By his grace, we commit ourselves with you to the bonds of marriage and the Christian home.

MINISTER: Will all of you, by God's grace, do everything in your power to uphold and care for these two persons in their marriage?

PEOPLE: We will.

MINISTER TO PARENTS: Will you give your blessing to (bride) and (groom) in their new relationship? Will you support them with the love and freedom they need? Will you share your experience and wisdom with them as they seek it, as you learn from them as well?

PARENTS: We will. We now reaffirm our continuing love for our child, and we recognize that henceforth our primary responsibility is to both of them together.

The Kiss

According to an old Scottish source, "The parson who presided over the marriage ceremony uniformly claimed it as his privilege to have a smack at the lips of the bride immediately after the performance of his official duties." This was supposed to secure the future happiness of the bride.

The Dollar Dance

The Polish custom of the dollar dance, which requires guests to pay a dollar to dance with the bride or groom, is intended to help the newlyweds pay for their honeymoon. Sometimes money is placed in a small white satin purse worn on the bride's waist; sometimes bills are pinned to the bride's dress; and sometimes coins are hurled at a plate set out specifically for that purpose. The dollar dance is performed at many weddings in the United States, regardless of the heritage of the bride and groom.

Shoes

Traditionally, shoes have been tied to or thrown at the newlyweds' getaway vehicle for good luck. This custom may be derived from any number of old practices that involve shoes. The ancient Assyrians and Hebrews gave a sandal as a token of good faith when closing a bargain or to signify the transfer of property. The ancient Egyptians exchanged sandals to indicate a transfer of property or granting of authority. It was customary to fling a sandal to the ground as a symbol of possession of the land, as demonstrated by this line from Psalm 60: "Upon the land of Edom do I cast my shoe." In old Britain, it was customary for the father of the bride to give the groom one of the bride's shoes as a token of the transfer of authority. The groom tapped the bride on the head with her shoe to impress her with her husband's new authority and position. The husband, for his part, was obliged to take an oath to treat his wife well.

Nowadays shoes are seldom tied to or thrown at departing newlyweds, but the custom lives on in the decorating of getaway cars with signs, balloons, and streamers.

Gifts

The popular tradition of throwing a bridal shower for a soon-to-be-married woman began in Holland. A bride would be showered with gifts if her father refused to provide her with a dowry. The shower custom spread to the United States, but it is not, for example, common in England.

According to an etiquette book published in 1907 by the New York Society of Self-Culture, wedding gifts have not always been common: "Wedding presents have now, in some instances, become almost gorgeous. The old fashion started amongst the frugal Dutch with the custom of providing the young couple with their household gear and a sum of money with which to begin their married life. It has now degenerated into a very bold display of wealth and ostentatious generosity, so that friends of moderate means are afraid to send anything. . . . In France they do things better—the nearest of kin subscribing a sum of money which is sent to the bride's mother, who invests it in good securities, in gold and silver, in the bridal trousseau, or in the furnishings of the house, as the good sense of all parties combine to direct."

Conclusion

Many wedding customs and beliefs that began hundreds or even thousands of years ago remain with us today in some form. Brides and grooms today participate in these old traditions with varying degrees of solemnity.

One thing all couples seem to have in common, though, is a need to incorporate something of the spiritual in their wedding ceremonies. The manner in which this need is manifested, naturally, depends on the environment and upbringing of the bride and groom. For some couples, a civil ceremony in a judge's chambers is quite enough. For others, a simple Quaker ceremony witnessed by friends is the most meaningful. Some couples feel that the warmth and familiarity of a home or garden wedding is the only way to go, and still other couples believe deeply that they wouldn't be married unless they were to walk down the aisle and be joined together in a church.

Whatever the prevailing customs and beliefs in your family or community, it is vital that you follow your hearts, are comfortable with your decisions, remain considerate of each other's feelings, hold fast to your own beliefs, and act kindly toward your family and friends. Follow the customs that you believe are important, and do not be afraid to make your wedding uniquely your own.

Appendix B: Recommended Resources

Bridal Fairs

The Great Bridal Expo: 800-422-3976; www.greatbridalexpo.com

General Information

The Knot: www.theknot.com

Jewelry

American Gem Society: 702-255-6500; www.ags.org; agsadam@aol.com

Tiffany and Company: 800-526-0649 for a free copy of the booklet *How to Buy a Diamond;* www.tiffany.com

Professional Associations

American Gem Society: 702-255-6500; www.ags.org; agsadam@aol.com

American Rental Association: 800-334-2177; www.ararental.org

American Society of Travel Agents: 703-739-2782; www.astanet.com; asta@astanet.com

The Association of Bridal Consultants: 860-355-0464; bridalassn@aol.com

The Association of Certified Professional Wedding Consultants: 408-223-5686

The Association for Wedding Professionals International: 800-242-4461; www.afwpi.com

International Special Events Society: 800-688-ISES; www.ISES.com

Leading Caterers of America: 800-743-6660; www.leadingcaterers.com

National Association of Catering Executives: www.nace.net

National Bridal Service: 804-355-6495; www.nationalbridalservice.com

National Limousine Association: 800-NLA-7007; info@limo.org

Travel

American Rental Association: 800-334-2177; www.ararental.org

American Society of Travel Agents: 703-739-2782; www.astanet.com;
asta@astanet.com

AMTRAK (US): 800-872-7245; www.amtrak.com

Anguilla Tourist Board: 800-553-4939

Antigua and Barbuda Tourist Office: 212-541-4117; www.antigua-barbu-da.org; info@antigua-barbuda.org

Aruba Tourism Authority: 800-TO-ARUBA; www.aruba.com

Australian Tourist Commission: 800-333-0262; www.australia.com

Austrian National Tourist Office: 212-575-7723; www.austria-tourism.at;
antonycsec@ibm.net

Bahamas Ministry of Tourism: 212-758-2777; 800-8-BAHAMAS;
www.bahamas.com

Barbados Tourism Authority: 800-221-9831; www.barbados.org

Belgian Tourist Office: 212-758-8130; www.visitbelgium.com

Brazilian Tourist Office: 212-997-4070

British Tourist Authority: 800-462-2748; www.btausa.com

Caribbean Tourism Organization: 212-635-9530; www.caribtourism.com

Curacao Tourist Board: 212-683-7660; www.curacao-tourism.com

Denmark Tourism Board: 212-885-9700; www.goscandinavia.com

Discover British Columbia: 800-663-6000

Disney's Fairy Tale Wedding: 407-363-6333

Florida Tourism: 904-487-1462

French Government Tourist Office: 212-838-7800;
www.francetourism.com

German National Tourist Office: 212-661-7200

Greek National Tourist Organization: 212-421-5777

Iceland Tourist Office: 212-885-9700; www.goscandinavia.com

Irish Tourist Board: 212-418-0800; www.ireland.travel.ie

Italian Government Travel Office: 212-245-5618 or 212-245-4882;
www.italiantourism.com

Kenya Consulate and Tourist Office: 212-486-1300;
www.africanvacation.com/kenya

Las Vegas Convention and Visitors Authority: 702-892-0711;
www.lasvegas24hours.com

Maui Visitors Bureau: 800-525-MAUI; www.visitmaui.com

Norwegian Tourist Board: 212-885-9700; www.goscandinavia.com

Philippines Department of Tourism: 212-575-7915; www.tourism.gov.ph

Pocono Mountains Vacation Bureau: 800-762-6667; www.poconos.org

RAIL EUROPE: 800-872-7245

Scottish Tourist Board: 031-332-2433

South African Tourism Board: 800-822-5368; www.satour.org

South Pacific Holidays: 800-877-SEEFIJI; www.spac.com

St. Maarten Tourist Office: 800-ST-MAARTEN; www.st-maarten.com

Swedish Tourism Board: 212-885-9700; www.goscandinavia.com

Swiss National Tourist Office: 212-757-5944;
www.switzerlandtourism.com

Tahiti Tourism Board: 310-414-8484; www.gototahiti.com

Tahoe North Visitors and Convention Bureau: 800-824-6348;
www.tahoefun.org

U.S. Virgin Islands Department of Tourism: 800-USVI-INFO

Wedding Attire

Discount Bridal Service: 800-874-8794; www.discountbridalservice.com

Glossary

ascot (AS-kot). A broad neck scarf knotted so that one end lies flat over the other; supposedly developed for wear at the Ascot horse races in England.

boutonniere (boo-tuh-NEER). A flower or flowers worn in a buttonhole, as of a lapel.

buffet (buh-FAY). A meal at which guests serve themselves from various dishes on a table or sideboard.

calligraphy (kuh-LIG-ruh-fee). The art of fine handwriting.

calling card. An engraved card bearing one's full name and sometimes one's address; used when making visits or when sending gifts. (Not to be confused with a business card.)

canapé (KAN-uh-pay). A cracker or small piece of bread served with a spread and served as an appetizer.

chutney (CHUT-nee). A pungent relish made of fruits, spices and herbs.

coat of arms. A group of emblems and figures, usually arranged on and around a shield, that serves as the insignia of a person, family, or institution.

cuff link. A fastening for a shirt cuff, usually made of two buttons or buttonlike parts connected with a chain or shank that passes through two slits in the cuff.

cummerbund (KUM-r-bund). Broad, pleated sash worn around the waist, pleats facing upward, with men's formal dress.

curry powder. A pungent blended condiment prepared from cumin, coriander, turmeric, and other spices.

cutaway. A man's formal daytime coat, with front edges sloping diagonally from the waist and forming tails at the back.

emboss. To carve or print a raised design.

fiancé (fee-ahn-SAY). A man engaged to be married.

fiancée (fee-ahn-SAY). A woman engaged to be married.

four-in-hand. A necktie tied in a slipknot with long ends left hanging one in front of the other.

French cuff. A wide cuff for a shirt sleeve that is folded back and fastened with a cuff link.

hors d'oeuvre (or-DURV). An appetizer served before a meal.

huppah (HUP-ah). A flowered arch or canopy placed over the bride and groom in Jewish ceremonies, symbolizing the home the couple will share.

informal. In reference to clothing: casual, unceremonious, relaxed, or designed for wear on everyday occasions. In reference to an event: not requiring formal dress, such as a tuxedo.

informals. Small foldover stationery cards, usually with a monogram or name printed on the front; used for handwritten thank-you notes and invitations to informal events.

mores (MOR-ayz). Customs that are considered conducive to the welfare of society and that through general observance sometimes develop the force of law.

open stock. Merchandise kept in stock to enable customers to replace or supplement articles purchased in sets; merchandise that will not be discontinued.

piqué (pih-KAY). A tightly woven fabric with raised patterns.

prie-dieu (pree-DYUH). A desklike kneeling bench with a ledge upon which a book may be rested.

R.S.V.P. Abbreviation of French phrase *répondez s'il vous plaît*, which means "answer if you please."

studs. A small ornamental button mounted on a short post for insertion through an eyelet, as on a dress shirt.

tails. A man's formal coat with long, tapering tails at the back.

thermography. A process for producing raised lettering, as on stationery, by application of a powder fused by heat to the fresh ink.

tiropitas. Phyllo dough filled with feta cheese; served as an appetizer.

waistcoat. A vest.

winged collar. A stiff stand-up collar with its corners turned down in front; worn by men in formal dress.

Storybook Weddings

by Robin Kring

Here are fifty wedding themes to help a bride and groom create a unique event that will be remembered well past the couple's golden anniversary. Included are creative, theme-appropriate ideas for invitations; fashions and costumes for the bride, groom, and the entire wedding party; décor and special touches for the ceremony and reception; and entertainment and menu concepts. Each special theme is designed to make for an unforgettable occasion.

Order #6010 $8.00

Something Old, Something New

by Becky Long

This book contains a treasure trove of ideas to create a most memorable wedding celebration. It includes innovative suggestions for everything from invitations and programs to decorations and keepsakes, intriguing wedding customs from around the world, original wedding themes, novel suggestions for rehearsal dinners and bridesmaids' luncheons, and a user-friendly reference guide to etiquette and budgeting time and money.

Order #6011 $9.95

Order Form

Qty.	Title	Author	Order No.	Unit Cost (U.S. $)	Total
	Best Baby Shower Book	Cooke, Courtney	1239	$7.00	
	Best Baby Shower Party Games #1	Cooke, Courtney	6063	$3.95	
	Best Baby Shower Party Games #2	Cooke, Courtney	6069	$3.95	
	Best Bridal Shower Party Games #1	Cooke, Courtney	6060	$3.95	
	Best Bridal Shower Party Games #2	Cooke, Courtney	6068	$3.95	
	Best Party Book	Warner, Penny	6089	$9.00	
	Best Wedding Shower Book	Cooke, Courtney	6059	$7.00	
	Dinner Party Cookbook	Brown, Karen	6035	$9.00	
	Games People Play	Warner, Penny	6093	$8.00	
	Pick A Party	Sachs, Patty	6085	$9.00	
	Pick-A-Party Cookbook	Sachs, Patty	6086	$11.00	
	Something Old, Something New	Long, Becky	6011	$9.95	
	Storybook Weddings	Kring, Robin	6010	$8.00	
				Subtotal	
				Shipping and Handling (see below)	
				MN residents add 6.5% sales tax	
				Total	

YES! Please send me the books indicated above. Add $2.00 shipping and handling for the first book with a retail price up to $9.99 or $3.00 for the first book with a retail price of over $9.99. Add $1.00 shipping and handling for each additional book. All orders must be prepaid. Most orders are shipped within two days by U.S. Mail (7–9 delivery days). Rush shipping is available for an extra charge. Overseas postage will be billed. **Quantity discounts available upon request.**

Send book(s) to:

Name _____ Address _____

City _____ State _____ Zip _____

Telephone (_____)_____

Payment via:

❑ Check or money order payable to Meadowbrook Press (No cash or CODs please)

❑ Visa (for orders over $10.00 only)   ❑ MasterCard (for orders over $10.00 only)

Account # _____ Signature _____

Exp. Date _____

A *FREE* Meadowbrook Press catalog is available upon request.
You can also phone or fax us with a credit card order.

Mail to: Meadowbrook Press
5451 Smetana Drive, Minnetonka, MN 55343
Toll-Free 800-338-2232

Phone 612-930-1100   Fax 612-930-1940

For more information (and fun) visit our website:
www.meadowbrookpress.com